Are You Good

Are You Good Enough?

From Crisis to Confidence in
15 Text Messages

Bill McFarlan and Dr Alex Yellowlees

CAPSTONE

Copyright © 2006 Bill McFarlan and Dr Alex Yellowlees

The right of Bill McFarlan and Dr Alex Yellowlees to be identified as the authors of this book has been asserted in accordance with the Copyright, Designs and Patents Act 1988

First published 2006 by
Capstone Publishing Limited (a Wiley Company)
The Atrium
Southern Gate
Chichester
West Sussex
PO19 8SQ
www.wileyeurope.com
Email (for orders and customer service enquires): cs-books@wiley.co.uk

CIP catalogue records for this book are available from the British Library and the US Library of Congress

ISBN-13: 978-1-84112-701-9
ISBN-10: 1-84112-701-9

Typeset in 10/13 pt Meridien by Sparks, Oxford – www.sparks.co.uk
Printed and bound in Great Britain by TJ International Ltd, Padstow, Cornwall

This book is printed on acid-free paper responsibly manufactured from sustainable forestry in which at least two trees are planted for each one used for paper production.

IMPORTANT!

Any resemblance between characters in this book and people you have met is entirely intentional. The names are made up – but the characteristics are real.

Get to know the people in this story and work out which traits they share with people you know.

There's a bit of us all in these characters. There's certainly a slice of the two of us in them!

Bill and Alex

Dedication

I would like to dedicate this book to my daughters Robyn and Rea who are a constant source of joy and inspiration.

Alex Yellowlees

To Victoria, Emma and Andrew. Sorry we were unaware of lots of the stuff in this book when you were born – but delighted to have passed on what your mum and I learned along the way.

Your confidence thrills me more than I can ever say.

Bill McFarlan

Contents

Acknowledgements

'The pizzas' (Chapter 3) is adapted from *Working with Eating Disorders and Self-Esteem* by Dr Alex Yellowlees and is based on *Self Care* by L. Keegan.

'The Confidence Compass' (Chapters 6 and 7) is adapted from 'The Self-Esteem Matrix' by Professor Chris Mruk.

'What do your words say about you?' (Chapter 11) is based on the principles of *Drop the Pink Elephant* by Bill McFarlan, first published by Wiley Capstone in 2003.

'Acting as if' (Chapter 13) and 'The Mind Map' (Chapter 14) are adapted from the work of Anthony Robbins.

The concept of self-esteem outlined in this book is based on the work of Nathaniel Branden.

A special thanks to Alex's daughter Robyn for her computer skills in developing the early draft of the manuscript illustrations.

And a big thanks to Bill's wife Caroline and daughter Victoria for their vigilant and thorough proofreading.

Foreword

When I first met Bill McFarlan back in 1991, we were both sports presenters on *BBC Breakfast News*. While it was clear Bill loved sport and TV, it was obvious even then that he had a much greater passion – helping people to build confidence.

Through his training courses and seminars, Bill had been drilling down for some years to find out what was at the core of the issue. When he met Dr Alex Yellowlees in 2001, he struck oil. Here was a psychiatrist who'd been working for 20 years to bring what he'd learned about self-esteem to the surface – and in Bill, he found the vehicle. Together, they formed a formidable duo: the confidence guru and the great communicator.

In an enlightening – yet gripping – manner, this remarkable book they've written together breaks new ground in explaining the complex issues that build and knock our confidence each day.

In *Are You Good Enough?* Bill and Alex share the secrets of how to look confident, act confidently – and most of all, become genuinely confident.

Enjoy the book.

All the best,

Eamonn Holmes

Preface

People in Britain have more choices than ever before … but are they any happier?

There's evidence to suggest that many are drowning under the weight of their responsibilities and losing confidence in their ability to juggle more and more tasks.

Steve and Lynn Clark are one such couple.

Married with a five-year-old child, they are successful and happy. On the surface.

But their relationship is beginning to stagnate and their confidence in their life together – and each other – is starting to crumble.

Until, that is, an unsolicited text message asks a searching question. It's the first of a series that causes them to question their behaviour and their values – and devise a series of remedies for their growing problems.

Together, they create new ways to build confidence. Rules that anyone can apply to their own lives with similar results.

Through this modern parable, told by Bill McFarlan – author of the best-selling *Drop the Pink Elephant* – and psychiatrist Dr Alex Yellowlees, one of Britain's foremost experts in confidence, the authors get to the root of issues that affect every adult across the UK.

Women feeling pressurised about their shape – over-achieving men who cannot enjoy success – parents who question if they're raising their kids well – partners who need to love themselves before they can love each other – adults who need to prune friends who are all 'take' and no 'give' – men and women who struggle to handle their relationship with their parents.

All these thorny issues are covered in a groundbreaking book that takes fact – rooted in medical knowledge – and applies it to today's society in a simple and straightforward manner. The dialogue is poignant, witty, heart-warming and real.

About the authors

Bill McFarlan

Bill McFarlan is Managing Director of The Broadcasting Business, one of Britain's leading media consultancies and communications training companies.

He works with leading companies across Europe, building the confidence of senior executives in dealing with television interviews and in making major announcements.

Bill's spent 30 years as a journalist and broadcaster, and is now the author of the best-selling communications handbook *Drop the Pink Elephant*, first published by Wiley Capstone in 2003.

He's presented TV programmes as diverse as *BBC Breakfast News* and *World's Strongest Man*.

Bill's a regular speaker at conferences and a passionate advocate of confidence-building techniques.

(The Broadcasting Business – 0141 427 2545, www.broadcastingbusiness.co.uk)

Dr Alex Yellowlees MB ChB MRCPsych MPhil

Dr Alex Yellowlees is Medical Director of the Priory Hospital, Glasgow.

He studied medicine at Edinburgh University and is a member of the Royal College of Psychiatrists.

Alex practises clinically as a consultant psychiatrist and has special expertise in the treatment of eating disorders.

Interested in the development of emotional health, he runs conferences, seminars and workshops on building self-confidence and maximizing personal potential.

(www.alexyellowlees.com)

Bill (left) and Alex working on *Are You Good Enough?* in Portugal

Together, Bill and Alex organize and present The Confident Company seminars (www.theconfidentcompany.biz), are co-founders of ConfidentScotland (www.confidentscotland.co.uk) and contribute to the Can-Do Scotland movement (www.can-do-scotland.co.uk).

Chapter I

Are you hungry for love?

Tuesday 27 September, early evening

Lynn opened a packet of smoky bacon crisps as she flopped on to the couch in front of the television. With her right hand, she dipped into the bag and with her left, lifted a full glass of Chardonnay to her lips.

Her high cheekbones were the focus of a pretty, friendly face. With dark, wavy, shoulder-length hair and striking hazel eyes, she continued to turn heads at 36 – and looked as if she would for some years to come.

But right now, an unwitting frown disturbed her forehead.

Something was niggling her.

Nicky, her five-year-old, was amusing himself with his PlayStation. He was a bright, enthusiastic boy. His blond hair and blue eyes often softened the hearts of shoppers who had initially stared in disapproval at his occasional supermarket tantrums.

Tonight, he was quiet and absorbed.

The peace was broken by the phone ringing. It was Steve, Lynn's husband of five years and partner for twice as long.

'Hi, Gorgeous!' he began. 'It's motorway mayhem. I'll try to be home by eight.'

'OK, Steve,' replied Lynn. 'Supper's on.'

Settling back on the couch, remote control in her hand, she spent the next 40 minutes hopping between soaps and reality TV.

A fight was breaking out in EastEnders. *An affair was smouldering in* Emmerdale.

A D-list celebrity was having a makeover. Britain's Worst Mum was screaming at her teenage daughter.

Desperate women queued up on the screen of Lynn's television to proclaim their increasing dissatisfaction with their figures. Lynn opened another packet of crisps as her frown deepened.

In Big Brother Revisited, *Emilie showed off the infected stud wound on her belly button and 20-year-old Karina talked about getting implants to enlarge her breasts.*

Nicky had by now lost any interest in his PlayStation and was seeking attention – but Lynn was tired. She knew it was time to bath him and get him ready for bed, but instead she hung on for a few minutes to watch the start of Extreme Makeovers, *as she opened a packet of biscuits.*

The pounds gained when Nicky was born had proved hard to shift. And recently, a carbohydrate fix won against another diet every time.

The diets she'd tried had worked – for a while. And then life would get in the way.

Lynn's mobile sounded from within her handbag with a message. Perhaps a text from Steve?

As she studied the screen, a puzzled look crossed her face.

A text message read:

> Are you hungry for love?

'Oh well, definitely not Steve.' She smiled. He used to send sexy texts, but not recently. They tended to be matter-of-fact arrangements, often enquiring what was for supper.

'So who's winding me up?' she mused.

The mobile was giving no clues as the text refused to reveal the sender.

'Must be a scam,' Lynn decided, as her attention wandered from the phone to the TV screen in front of her.

An advert for a new reality show began:

'Are you hungry for love? You could be one of ten contestants seeking the perfect partner on your very own Love Island …'

Lynn sat rooted to the TV screen – and glanced again at the text message.

'ARE YOU HUNGRY FOR LOVE?' it confirmed. Her puzzled thoughts were interrupted by the sound of Steve's key in the door.

'Hi, Gorgeous!' said Steve, pecking Lynn on the cheek.

'How's my boy?' he enquired, ruffling Nicky's already tousled hair.

Steve reached for the remote and flicked to the Champions League football.

He was youthful for his age. With his milestone 40th fast approaching, only a little grey hair around the temples betrayed any real sign of ageing.

He'd always had smile lines around his eyes – one of the clues to his character that had attracted Lynn to him a decade ago. Now, however, more worry lines below his mop of fair hair suggested his troubled thoughts at times outnumbered his carefree moments.

His blue eyes were always searching the room, normally seeking out the next one-liner.

His lack of opportunity to play five-a-side football remained a constant irk and an explanation for the paunch now protruding above his belt.

'Steve, did you send me a text?' asked Lynn.

'No, I phoned to say it was mayhem on the motorway,' he replied, somewhat defensively.

'No, I don't mean that. I got this strange message a few minutes ago,' she retorted.

Steve's mildly surprised expression barely disguised his greater interest in the football than in his wife's puzzling experience.

'It just read: "ARE YOU HUNGRY FOR LOVE?"' she persisted.

'It'll be some kind of advertising or a scam,' offered Steve, his eyes fixed to the TV screen.

'Well I thought so,' said Lynn, 'but then an advert began on TV with exactly the same words.'

A sharp intake of breath from Steve caused Lynn to look back to her husband. But he was reacting to a header whistling past the keeper's unguarded left post.

'Steve, are you listening?' she asked.

'Of course,' he replied. 'You got a text about a TV show.'

'Well I don't think it was connected,' she insisted.

'Probably a new way of marketing TV,' Steve replied. 'It's very sophisticated these days, you know.'

'But how did that text arrive seconds before it came up on the telly?' she persisted.

'I've no idea, Lynn. Anyway, what's for supper? I'm starving,' insisted Steve.

Now it was her turn to be distracted. She looked forward to Steve coming home each night, but her conversation these days seemed of less interest to him than the big football matches. Correction – any football match!

'What are we having?' asked Steve again.

'Spaghetti Bolognese. But I'm not particularly hungry,' replied Lynn.

'You've been at these crisps again,' was Steve's insightful response; he lifted the near-empty family pack wrapper accusingly.

'Well I never know when you'll be home,' hit back Lynn. 'And I'm hungry long before you sit down to eat.'

'No point complaining about piling on the pounds, then,' Steve replied, less than helpfully.

If anything bothered Lynn it was her weight. From being a size 10 before Nicky's birth, she was now a 12. Hard to imagine that at one time she'd been an 8. Most of her clothes were too tight for her and every time she stood in front of the mirror, she felt depressed and disgusted.

She knew this wasn't the 'puppy fat' her mother had so often teased her about in her teenage years. This seemed determined to stay and scream at her, every time she looked at her reflection.

The love-hate food relationship

Lynn's in conflict with food

And she **constantly** worries over what she's eating.

Sometimes it's simply at the back of her mind as she negotiates her way through another busy day … but often it dominates the forefront of her attention, to the extent of being an intense and distressing preoccupation.

There are just so many questions and concerns buzzing around in her head all the time:

'What to eat – how much – and how often?'

'What size of helping should I have – how many calories does that contain – just how "fattening" is this?'

'What will be the result of eating this – and how will I feel afterwards if I do?'

'If I eat this now, will it go straight to my waist, hips, thighs or my bum – and can I find the time to "work it off" tomorrow?'

'Will the cellulite on my thighs make them look like orange peel?'

And so on. And on. And *on* it goes!

These are just some of the myriad worries at the back of Lynn's mind, sapping her energy and taking the edge off her pleasure in eating.

Robbing her of some of the joy in life itself.

To eat or not to eat?

Make no mistake about it – *Lynn* **loves** *food*!

And she really enjoys preparing meals for others.

For her, it is an expression of her love for her family, for Steve and Nicky.

However, since she was a teenager, Lynn has become increasingly **wary** *of food*.

She's become fearful of eating too much during a meal – even unsure what 'too much' really is.

She's also concerned about eating the 'wrong things' and at the 'wrong time' of day.

Every TV programme she watches seems to be sending her messages that she should lose weight or that she needs to change her body in one way or another.

Glossy magazines propounding the crazy world of the 'Eating Secrets of the Supermodels' have virtually taken up residence in her doctor's surgery waiting room, somehow lending a degree of credibility to their confusing and conflicting dieting claims.

On occasions it all becomes 'too much' to take in.

Unable to reach a decision about what to eat, she often decides to eat nothing at all and skips lunch instead.

To her disgust, by evening she is sometimes so hungry she ends up overeating while watching TV.

Diet-crazy

Lynn sometimes wonders if the world has gone diet-crazy.

But then she reminds herself that all her friends are dieting too. So it 'must be OK ... mustn't it'?

Steve's already joked that new diets were being created deep underground during the night, only to emerge at daybreak in the morning newspaper, in order to give Lynn the magic answer to all her weight worries: the quick, easy and hassle-free way to lose weight.

Lynn tends to feel 'at her fattest' just before going on holiday with Steve.

She'd love to be able to fit into the new red bikini she's bought, and wants to look good on the beach and by the pool.

Comfort eating

Lynn snacks on crisps and packets of biscuits when she feels tired and fed up.

She's *comfort eating* by using food as a way of trying to change the way she feels at a particular moment.

It's an understandable attempt to boost her flagging energy after an exhausting day at work, further depleted by looking after demanding Nicky.

It also helps to lift her mood.

However, Lynn's unhappy not only about her weight and shape, but also about the current state of her relationship with Steve.

Comfort eating provides her with a way of feeling better – quickly.

And it works!

But here's the catch – *only for a while.*

Soon after overeating, Lynn feels annoyed and even disgusted with herself and within a few days or weeks she goes on yet another diet.

Emotional hunger

Lynn's pattern of spells of comfort eating, followed by the adoption of the next dieting fad she comes across in a glossy magazine, is her way of trying to feel better and happier about herself *in general*.

In fact, Lynn's comfort eating is an attempt to fill an inner emptiness or vacuum – to satisfy a form of *emotional hunger*.

This sense of emotional emptiness is being created by the absence of real self-love and a more loving and satisfying relationship with Steve.

Lynn took a copy of Zest *magazine to bed with her while Steve watched the late night Champions League highlights – despite his impending early-morning monthly sales meeting.*

Restlessly, she flicked through a piece about comfort eating, but quickly put it down.

'Are you hungry for love?' she considered again.

Was it a secret admirer? Chance would be a fine thing!

She felt less attractive than ever. And Steve's obvious lack of interest only confirmed her feelings.

She was sure he still loved her, but it would be nice if he would show it just once in a while.

Still, she wasn't one of those women who comfort ate, Lynn told herself. She just snacked because she was hungry.

She was hungry for food, not hungry for love.

Or so she thought.

Chapter 2

Are you good enough?

Wednesday 28 September, 7.07 a.m.

Steve looked smart in his dark blue suit as he kissed Lynn on the cheek and shouted goodbye to his son.

The thin smile he wore for his wife quickly melted as his attention turned to the meeting in 53 minutes' time.

This time last year, Steve had enjoyed the monthly regional sales conference calls. But then, this time last year, Steve was about to be anointed Regional Sales Director of the Year.

His boss, Dave Curtis, was biting into a blueberry muffin when Steve entered the conference room.

'Morning,' offered Steve, brightly.

'Morning,' was Dave's monotone reply, his eyes fixed in the centre of his cake.

Dave could ill-afford early morning muffins, with a stomach that completely hid his belt.

He was hunched over the desk, with layers of fat at the back of his massive neck gathering like ripples on a wind-swept pond.

The meeting began courteously enough as the company's eight UK regional centres exchanged greetings.

The overall picture was bright, with one exception. And Dave wasn't about to let it pass.

'Steve, perhaps you could explain to everyone why we're bucking the trend here,' he began, unexpectedly.

Steve paused. He could feel the heat build under his freshly ironed shirt collar. He could hear the silence that seemed to last forever, disturbed only by his heart thumping loudly.

'Well, we're experiencing flat sales this quarter,' he began.

'And why?' pressed Dave, chewing deep into his muffin.

'Difficult to say,' offered Steve.

'Well let me try,' continued Dave, looking straight ahead, well away from Steve's gaze. 'We have a Sales Director of the Year, resting on his laurels … a demotivated sales team under him … and an unimpressed client base. Fair comment, Steve?'

'I'm not resting on my laurels,' replied Steve weakly. 'I've been …'

'You've been basking in the glory of your award instead of …'

'I've not been basking in any glory,' interrupted Steve angrily.

Now Dave had his undivided attention, he had his prey fixed in his beady stare.

'I'm not finished,' he barked. 'You're only as good as your last sale, Steve. Or in your case, your last lost order. The figures need to improve – and improve fast.'

Steve was stunned to silence and sat chided and humiliated for the rest of the meeting, as Dave waxed lyrical about his plans to turn things round.

But Steve wasn't listening. He was slowly dying of embarrassment, imagining the reaction around the company to the tongue-lashing Dave had handed him.

Why could he never win an argument with Dave? Why did he feel pathetic whenever criticized severely? It was as if he lost the power of speech, which he found so exhilarating in meetings with clients.

He had got on so well with his old boss, Craig. Even when sales were flat in the second quarter last year, Craig had remained uncritical. He had certainly, privately, pointed out some improvements Steve could make to his methods, but he did it so encouragingly that Steve had found it uplifting. His old boss had real integrity.

Craig would remind him that he remained a good salesman – and insisted that if he continued to believe in Steve, the least Steve could do was to agree.

Dave was silent as he walked out to leave his Regional Sales Director alone with his thoughts in the conference room.

Steve stared at the wall, playing the conversation over again in his mind.

The sharpness of Dave's tone reminded him of just one person. His father.

Steve had produced great work at school in his early teens. A stunning 91% in English in his second year.

And what did his dad say?

'Where did you drop the 9%?'

He felt so deflated, after looking forward to receiving his dad's warm approval. His mother said it was just his dad's way. But it made no difference to young Steven.

Even when he'd pointed out that he was second in the class, his father had demanded to know who had beaten him.

'Gary Wilson?' his father had sneered. 'Didn't think you'd be trailing him.'

Then there was the embarrassment of Saturdays. Sure, his dad came to the school football matches, but he always ended up arguing with the ref – when he wasn't yelling at his son to 'run with the ball – don't just kick it away, Steven.'

'All I needed in the pouring rain, 3–0 down and already being screamed at by my captain,' Steve recollected, 'was for my dad to join the commentary team!'

His dad had reacted even more discouragingly as Steve started to act as the class joker in response to being called a 'swot'. Ironically, he became more popular at school – and less popular with his dad at home.

Despite reasonable leaving certificate grades, his dad had by that stage repeatedly branded his son as 'not the sharpest knife in the drawer'.

One of Steve's female sales team broke the silence when entering the room to inform him there was a call.

'Tell them I'll call back,' he snapped.

'Don't you want to take it,' suggested Fiona. 'It's …'

'I don't care if it's the Prime Minister. Tell him I'll call back!'

Steve could barely look in Dave's direction as he marched to the car park to drive to his first call of the day. He caught sight of his silver Ford Mondeo and felt another shiver of disgust.

His pride and joy – the 5-series BMW – was demanded back at the end of the previous month as he was awarded the car that reflected his success.

'A bloody Mondeo,' he muttered to nobody in particular.

Sitting on the passenger seat was a copy of the morning paper, the back page dominated by just one word: 'Superflops!'

The 'Superflops' in question were his beloved United, whose expensive players had gone down 2–0 the previous evening to Fulham. He always felt bad even the day after a United defeat, but this season they were winning only one game in four.

Loyally, he would turn up every second Saturday as a season ticket holder, if only to hurl abuse at the players he idolized.

Still, these guys were paid a fortune to take the knocks when they deserved it. And they deserved it right now.

Steve had a sneaking feeling that he also deserved the criticism. But then, he felt that even when there was none.

He flicked through the paper from the back, dwelling for a moment on the recruitment section, before speeding out the car park and on to the dual carriageway.

— — — ▬ ■

Steve deserves better!

How highly we rate ourselves as people affects our day-to-day sense of happiness and satisfaction with ourselves and our lives.

But just how well and how accurately we carry out this self-rating depends on our inner sense of *self-worth.*

This is important because our sense of self-worth influences our choices, our outlook on life and our attitude towards ourselves and others. In other words, our happiness.

Some people rate themselves so poorly that they simply feel *'not good enough'* for life itself. They go about their daily lives harbouring a deep sense of inner unworthiness and hoping that no one will find out how awful they really feel inside.

Many successful individuals who are held in high regard by their colleagues and friends inwardly hide a painful sense of inadequacy and inferiority.

The true value we place on ourselves is deeply connected to what we feel about ourselves on the *inside* and less to do with how others see us from the *outside*.

This inner rating of our personal value is the *judgement* we pass on ourselves – rather than what other people think of us.

We live our lives with the sentence we pass on ourselves.

Good enough for life

Outwardly, Steve is a successful man. He is very good at his job.

After all, last year he was awarded the title of Regional Sales Director of the Year. His ex-boss valued him highly and Lynn clearly sees him as a success and tells him so openly.

But here is the problem.

Steve believes that he is a *failure*.

He's dissatisfied with his achievements and continues to strive after 'more success', as he puts it, so that he can 'relax'. He believes that only then will he be satisfied with his life.

But the reality is that he will never find 'enough success' because deep down he does not feel '*good enough*' about himself.

Although he has always been a high achiever, his sense of self-worth remains poor.

An active man, always on the move, he has become a fugitive from himself, 'on the run' from his inner sense of inadequacy.

This is the case with so many over-achievers who drive themselves on to higher and higher levels of personal accomplishment in an unconscious attempt to discover a satisfactory level of self-worth.

The stamp of approval

For most of us, our sense of self-worth is nurtured to a great extent by our parents.

The experience of being loved unconditionally by them as children, simply for being alive, lies at the very heart of healthy self-esteem.

Often without realizing it, parents lay the foundation stone for our opinion of ourselves.

If we feel loved and valued by them in our own right, we absorb this emotional nectar and use it to feed our developing sense of self – of who we are.

In this way, as we grow up, we begin to develop a sense of being *'good enough for life'*.

This includes feeling loved, loveable, of value and of significance.

The possession of such a sense of basic self-worth is an inner gold-mine as we face the challenges of life.

Steve felt as if he had to earn his father's approval, constantly. And that his father's love and acceptance were conditional on his school achievements.

He never felt that his best was ever really 'good enough' for his dad.

Steve also experienced his father as being very critical. He felt that, however hard he might try, he could never please him.

As a result, he never felt validated by his father as his 'worthy son'.

Steve never fully experienced his father's **stamp of approval**.

Heading for a crisis

Steve's self-worth is based too heavily on the *outside world* in order to compensate for the fact that deep down *inside* he rates himself so poorly.

Currently Steve measures his worth in terms of his:

- Career

- Car

- Football team, and

- Charm

He feels only as good as his last sale, the size and make of his car, the success of his football team and his ability to charm the opposite sex.

Superficially confident, Steve can behave like the life and soul of the party, flirting excessively with female colleagues.

He works and plays hard, driving both himself and his car fast.

And this strategy for boosting his poor sense of self-worth works.

But here's the catch – only for as long as the outside world plays the game.

And in real life, it rarely does.

He's recently experienced a change of boss. Currently, Dave is less supportive and openly critical. He may even be trying to bring him down, perhaps because he is threatened by Steve's successful reputation and good relationship with his predecessor.

In addition, female colleagues in the sales team, whom Steve has charmed so effectively in the past, are now talking about leaving the company because he has recently become much more unreasonable and demanding.

United, the football team he has supported so faithfully for many years, is now 'letting him down' and beginning to fail.

And to top it all, his pride and joy, his company car, the BMW, has been downgraded to what he views as a lesser set of wheels, a Ford Mondeo.

His outer world is coming apart at the seams and, as a result, his inner world is beginning to crumble.

Without realizing it, Steve is moving rapidly towards a personal crisis.

— — — — ▓

Steve straightened his shoulders and strode confidently into his customer's office. Despite feeling fed up, he certainly wasn't going to show it.

The customer, however, was running late, so Steve returned to his car to browse the paper for 15 minutes.

His phone bleeped and a message lit the screen:

Are you good enough?

Steve found Lynn's message untimely and unhelpful. He pressed 'reply' to tell her as much, but nothing happened. He tried several more times, but the message remained on screen.

Attempts to find out where it came from ended in failure.

Further annoyed that he'd jumped to conclusions about Lynn, he threw down the phone in frustration and lifted the paper.

A small advert in the bottom left-hand corner of the recruitment page caught his eye with the question it posed:

'Are you good enough to lead our small but dedicated sales team?'

'Good question!' he told himself.

A couple of pints took the edge off his stress on the way home that night, after what had been an awful day.

His calls had been, at best, unpromising and the morning's public humiliation was still on his mind.

He chatted with the barmaid at the Jug and Claret about nothing in particular. She seemed to like his style, his quick-fire humour and his smile. At least he hadn't lost his touch with the girls.

'Hi, Gorgeous!' he greeted his wife on the hands-free from the car. 'It's motorway mayhem, as ever. I'll try to be home by eight.'

Nicky was in bed when Steve returned, Lynn having had enough of her son's teatime tantrums.

Over a steak and kidney pie, Steve volunteered that he'd received one of Lynn's text scams:

'What – are you hungry for love?' enquired Lynn.

'No. Are you good enough?' replied Steve.

'Good enough?' said Lynn. 'At what?'

'God knows. I thought I was doing OK – but my boss disagrees. Craig was so different. We got on so well – my figures were ter-

rific – he was happy. But even when sales were lower, he was never on my back like Dave. He was encouraging, optimistic. He reminded me I was good at my job and with hard work, we'd get there.'

'You're still good at your job, Steve,' said Lynn.

'Doesn't feel like it,' Steve replied, 'especially with Dave breathing down my neck. But, you know, even last year when we were flying high, I just knew it was going to come to an end. I stood there in Disneyworld enjoying the fruits of my labour, and what do you think I was thinking?'

'What? Wish I could go on Thunder Mountain again?'

'No. Be serious. I was thinking: this is as good as it gets – and it's all downhill from here.'

'Steve, you're never happy!'

'No Lynn, I just want to succeed.'

'But you are a success. How much success do you want?'

'More than this.'

'Why?'

'So I can relax.'

'But you've just said that in Disneyworld, when Nicky and I were having the holiday of a lifetime, you were dreading the future.'

Steve had no answer.

▬ ▬ ▬ ▬ ▬

Chapter 3

Is your emotional bank balance in the red?

— — — ■ ▇

Friday 14 October, 8.45 a.m.

Lynn's mobile displayed 'MUM' as she began to answer the call while negotiating a tight parking space, much further away from her office than she'd wanted.

'Hello, dear,' began a friendly voice. 'Can you bring me a few bits and pieces on the way home tonight?'

Lynn had occasionally attempted to explain to her 71-year-old mother that collecting Nicky from school, picking up 'a few bits and pieces', taking the shopping to her miles off her route home and cooking dinner required the skills of a circus juggler!

But today, as usual, she just bit her lip and reached for a pen and paper. A driver blared his horn impatiently as she paused in her parking manoeuvre, causing her to jump.

That evening

It was after 6.30 before she delivered the 27 items of groceries to her mother – and an hour later before she got home.

The phone was ringing as she put her key in the door. It was Steve, with his customary call to say he was running late. 'Motorway mayhem' had cost him more than an hour. The rest of the delay was caused by the two unmentioned pints he'd downed before setting off.

He was winding up the call when 'CALL WAITING' interrupted – causing Lynn to rush her goodbyes as she took the new call.

'Lynn, it's Helena', began a faltering voice. 'I'm needing a sympathetic ear and a large glass of wine. Can I pop round?'

Lynn could have screamed. Instead, she said, 'Of course. I'll get Nicky off to bed and put some wine in the fridge.'

Feeling resentful of a free Friday evening now about to be swallowed up – and annoyed at her inability to turn Helena down – Lynn picked up the mail and began to open up the top letter, postmarked HSBC.

The bank statements often filled her with dread, but this one was especially unwelcome as her eye went straight to the heading on the unfriendly-looking letter.

It read: 'Account Overdrawn'.

With virtually no bonus money these past six months from Steve's disappointing order book, they were struggling financially. Worse still, Steve would be upset by the news.

Nicky was remonstrating by now – tired, hungry and starved of his mother's undivided attention.

Three times she begged him to put down the opened carton of orange juice he'd removed from the fridge, which she'd left ajar when popping in the wine. But when he finally dropped it – spilling orange juice in all directions – her reaction surprised him.

Her eyes filled and a solitary tear ran down each cheek.

The distinctive tone of an incoming text message came from her handbag on the kitchen table. At first, Lynn ignored it. But, drying her eyes, she reached into the bag and illuminated the phone.

The message read:

> Is your emotional bank balance in the red?

Lynn burst into tears.

— — — ▬ ■

People pleasers

Lynn is struggling to keep her hectic life in balance.

She's constantly bombarded by the demands of others.

In her work as a Human Resources trainer in the bank, she's repeatedly encouraging people to perform better – while often struggling herself.

At times she feels as if the needs of others are impossible to fulfil – like a bottomless pit!

And then there are Steve and Nicky to look after.

Steve plays little part in nurturing Nicky, preferring to deal with the 'nice' aspects of parenting, like taking him to the cinema or playing football in the park.

He avoids the 'tough' stuff such as keeping him in order. Certainly the 'messy' bits are usually left for Lynn to deal with.

Lynn finds herself taking on the responsibility for others all too easily.

She's done this for as long as she can remember. She recalls that her mother used to do the same.

Lynn learned this way of functioning from her as she was growing up.

Gradually, over the years, Lynn has become a **people pleaser** – without ever realizing it.

Guilt trips

Lynn also has an over-developed sense of responsibility. For everything.

If needed, she is there for family, friends, co-workers and indeed anyone who might seek her help or support.

Sometimes Steve says to her that she imagines being needed, even when she isn't.

Lynn finds herself unable to say '**no**', to anything or anybody.

If she does occasionally withhold her help, usually because she has simply taken on too much, she feels uncomfortable, uneasy and anxious.

As if somehow she is being '**selfish**'.

In other words, she goes on a guilt trip.

In error, Lynn has come to believe it's her job in life to please everyone and to ensure that others are happy by always putting **their** needs before her own.

Avoiding confrontation if she possibly can, she hates falling out with people because she likes to be liked.

More than that, Lynn **needs** to be liked.

This is because underneath the people pleaser coat she wears, Lynn is really an **approval seeker** in disguise.

Approval seekers have a deep and powerful desire for both themselves and their behaviour to be fully accepted by others.

The cycle works like this:

- If they are **needed** by others then they feel **liked**.

- If they are **liked** then they feel **approved** of.

- And if they gain **approval** they **feel better** about themselves.

Your emotional bank balance

The important upside for Lynn is that this pattern of functioning is a way of repeatedly giving little boosts to her fragile sense of self-worth.

The downside is that she has to keep on doing it over and over again for it to work.

The result:

Lynn ends up feeling utterly drained.

She's literally being sapped of energy by the incessant demands made by Nicky, Steve, her work and her friends.

And to top it all, her ageing mother is piling on the pressure through emotional blackmail.

The energy she **gives out** to others well exceeds the energy she **gets back** from those around her.

And that can only go on for so long before her battery runs flat.

Although Lynn has managed like this for years, she's gradually making too many withdrawals from her energy account.

Lynn's emotional bank balance is moving into the red.

— — — ◼

When Lynn answered the door, it was clear to anybody that she had been crying.

Except, that is, Helena Stoddart – a redhead with all the empathy of a cauliflower.

Her professional career as a criminal lawyer was as successful as her love life was disastrous.

'Sorry, Helena,' began Lynn, explaining her appearance, 'I've been a bit upset.'

'I'll give you upset,' shot back Helena. 'D'you know I got a message from Mark this morning on my voicemail – my bloody voicemail – more or less telling me it was over ...'

Helena didn't listen to Lynn's words of consolation as she tossed her coat on to the coach and, uninvited, took two large wine glasses down from the cabinet. All while recounting her latest love disaster.

Lynn could hear Nicky whimpering from the bedroom, possibly because she'd skipped the bedtime story to tidy up ahead of Helena's arrival. She could barely take in Helena's tale of woe as guilt consumed her to the point of drowning.

Steve arrived just 15 minutes later, to find Helena holding court in his flat, on her second glass of wine – with Nicky's whimper now upgraded to full-blown crying.

He allowed himself a brief, disappointed sigh at the sight of one of Lynn's 'bloodsucker' friends, as he called them, before going to attend to his son.

There were three bloodsuckers in all – the 'Three Witches' was the collective term he gave them. He just couldn't understand why she tolerated them.

Steve fell asleep on Nicky's tiny bed and, later on, found Helena leaving as he emerged from the dark bedroom.

'I'm sorry, Steve,' was Lynn's response, after closing the door. 'She's really upset. What could I do?'

'Tell her to bugger off and cry on somebody else's shoulder,' he volunteered, accepting that the remark would be met with a disapproving look.

'I put a couple of pizzas in the oven,' said Lynn. 'They should be ready.'

As Steve poured them both the remains of the second bottle of Chardonnay, Lynn told him about her latest text.

'Is your emotional bank balance in the red?' she offered. 'It really upset me. Well that and the thought of Helena using up my Friday night – having already spent an hour and a half getting mum's shopping and running round there!'

Steve looked down on the two uninviting cheese and tomato pizzas in front of them.

With his knife, he started to slice his pizza into quarters.

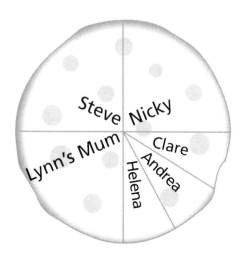

'Imagine this is all the energy you give to the people closest to you in your life, Lynn,' he began.

One quarter, you give to me. One quarter, you give to Nicky. One quarter, you give to your mum.'

'That's not true,' replied Lynn. 'Mum's 71 and ...'

'Just bear with me,' reasserted Steve.

'Now you've got one-quarter of your energy left. Who do you give it to?'

'Helena, Clare and Andrea,' she offered.

'Correct – the Three Witches.'

'Steve!'

'Now, Lynn, which of your close friends or relatives is, therefore, denied any of your energy?'

Lynn thought for a moment.

'Harriet?'

'No!'

'Carol?'

'No! And you're out of time!' said Steve triumphantly. 'It's you, Lynn. You have no energy left for yourself!'

That old chestnut. God knows how many times Steve had urged her to go back to dancing, take up yoga, learn to play tennis. Anything for herself. But she never had time.

'And where do I find the time for that, Einstein?' asked Lynn, a little sarcastically.

'Well, watch closely,' said Steve – now slicing up Lynn's pizza.

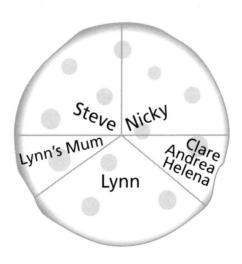

'Even if you give Nicky and me the same slice of your energy, if you just cut down a bit on your mum and halve – or better still – remove the Three Witches' slices – hey presto, you have some left over for you.'

Steve was on a roll. So he continued.

'Ask yourself what they all give to you. Your mum devours your time when it suits her – and you get virtually nothing back from the Witches. If you only gave any of them back what they give you, that would surely be fair wouldn't it?'

But how could she? Her mum had become increasingly dependent on Lynn since the death of her husband. And the Witches – no, Helena, Clare and Andrea – were equally demanding.

She could, however, see Steve's point. Very clearly, as it happened.

'But what has all that to do with my emotional bank balance being in the red?' she asked.

'You're overdrawn,' said Steve, 'because you're giving much more to your family and friends than you ever get back!'

— — — ▬ ▰

Chapter 4

who are the bullies in your life?

━ ━ ━ ━ ▇

Monday 17 October, 11.20 a.m.

Steve shook his client's hand after what had been a great meeting. The deal they'd concluded would shut his boss up for a while. He looked forward to witnessing the silence.

Steve's phone rang, displaying 'BULLDOG'.

It was his unflattering nickname for his boss.

'Hi, Dave,' he answered. 'Just going to call you with some good news.'

'That's funny,' replied the Bulldog. 'Just when I was calling you with some bad news.'

'What bad news?' asked Steve, his stomach tightening.

'Only a complaint from our biggest customer,' continued Dave '… about your drinking habits.'

Steve was speechless.

'I don't know what you're talking about,' began Steve, eventually.

'Well, I'll fill you in when I see you here at six,' snapped back Dave, before hanging up.

From his high of just two minutes ago, Steve now felt sick.

'Drinking habits?' he questioned to himself.

He sensed that the issue might have something to do with the smell of his lunchtime pints on his breath. But a bout of self-justification left him building a sense of indignation about the accusation. He was entitled to have a pint at lunchtime like anybody else, wasn't he? And he would tell Dave that to his face.

Steve pressed Lynn's number to speak to a friendly voice, but a text lit up his screen instead:

> who are the bullies in your life?

Steve looked around him, expecting to see somebody who had witnessed his call with the Bulldog. A mother was passing with her toddler. A construction worker, sitting on scaffolding, was biting into a sandwich.

To his surprise, the call connected to Lynn.

'Hi, Steve. How are you?'

For the second time in as many minutes, Steve was stunned to silence.

'Steve. Are you OK?' asked Lynn nervously.

'Lynn, did you just send me a text about bullies?' he eventually asked.

'Not me,' she replied. 'What about bullies?'

'Who are the bullies in your life?' Steve responded.

'Well, Dave for one,' began Lynn.

'For one?' questioned Steve. 'Who else?'

'Well, your dad, Steve,' was the blunt reply.

'Now, don't speak ill of the dead, Lynn,' said Steve.

'Well, you asked, Steve. You know he always bullied you. And you know he's still doing it from beyond the grave.'

Steve knew she was right. But the part of him that loved his dad refused to concede to the other part that resented him.

They spoke for several minutes about Dave's call. Steve felt a bit better. Lynn was right – Dave was nothing but a bully. Yet he seemed powerless to tell the Bulldog to back off.

A couple of lunchtime pints took his mind off the six o'clock meeting. Another couple at five helped relax him enough to reach Dave's office a little less nervous than he'd imagined.

To erase the smell of alcohol, he consumed the remainder of the packet of Polo Mints he'd used all week to keep the distinct odour of lunchtime beer from his customers.

Steve was barely in Dave's office when the Bulldog barked.

'Arriving at customers' premises reeking of booze is unprofessional,' started Dave.

'Who's complaining of that?' asked Steve defiantly.

'Peter Wilson of Dawsons,' came the quick reply.

'That uptight prat,' hit back Steve.

'Yes, otherwise known as Your Biggest Customer,' snapped Dave. 'And if he would like you to abstain for the next ten years and drink only milk, I would suggest you do it.'

'Since when was there a law saying you couldn't have a pint at lunchtime?' replied Steve, deciding to dig in.

'There isn't one,' came back Dave. 'Just as there isn't a law saying you can't sack a so-called Sales Director whose customers have stopped buying from him.'

'Sort it out, Steve. Now. And by the way, I've had one of your staff complaining about the way you're treating the girls in your team. I suggest you sort that out too … because nobody likes a bully.'

'Me, a bully?' exploded Steve. 'It's not me who's the bully.'

'Why – who else is?' demanded Dave.

Steve paused for a second and stared right into Dave's eyes.

'Well?' demanded the Bulldog.

Only it wasn't Dave that Steve saw. It was his father, demanding an explanation as to why he'd lost his house key.

'Well?' his father pressed.

Steve left Dave's office without speaking, almost knocking over Vicky from his team.

'Can I have a word tomorrow?' she shouted after him.

'Only if I can have a sale from you tomorrow,' growled back Steve.

All the way home, Steve's mind flicked between his boss and his father.

'You're not the sharpest knife in the drawer,' sniped his father, 'are you, Steven?'

His father would always wait just long enough for an answer to his rhetorical question before allowing Steven to go. Young Steven would stand there transfixed, never sure whether to defend himself or agree.

Whenever he had stood up for himself, his father would just grow angrier and sustain the attack. So, Steven learned that submission made the pain disappear quicker.

Only it didn't disappear. It just hid at the back of his mind until incidents like today's with Dave.

There he was, aged 39, unable to answer, unable to defend himself. So what did he do? He just ran away, like he used to when he was 9.

Steve had a blinding headache when he arrived back at the flat, brought on by the row, the driving rain and the difficulty of seeing through his watery eyes. He knew he needed glasses, but he wasn't ready to give in to middle age, as he saw it, just yet.

Two aspirins and a beer from the fridge had been consumed by the time Lynn walked through the door with Nicky.

'You're home early,' said Lynn, clearly with some pleasure.

'Yeah, well, traffic was lighter tonight,' offered Steve, unwilling to give a full explanation. 'Nicky, clear up all those toys before dinner,' he continued.

'You might at least say "hello" to him first,' reprimanded Lynn.

'Look, whose side are you on, Lynn?' snapped Steve.

'I'm not on any side,' she retorted.

'Well, you never discipline him, Lynn – and you don't back me up when I do, either,' fired back Steve.

'I just don't think you can treat your five-year-old son like one of your junior sales staff,' replied Lynn. 'Not that you should be treating them that way in the first place!'

Steve said nothing, but the words hit a raw nerve after Dave's accusation. He picked up his paper and strode through to his bedroom to channel hop, alighting accidentally on the latest goal to sink his beloved United. He switched off in disgust.

Steve just sat staring at the blank screen, rerunning the vivid and depressing events of the day. The phone call from Dave, the stormy meeting in his office and now the row with his wife.

— — — ▬ ▓

Being bullied

Steve is struggling with the agonizing mixture of feelings he's experiencing as a result of being bullied at the hands of Dave the Bulldog.

That sickening, churning sensation deep in the pit of his stomach is a poisonous cocktail of fear, hurt and rage.

The experience of being bullied can make us feel ill, both physically and emotionally. It's happening for Steve like this:

- *Fear* arises because Dave the Bulldog does have a degree of actual power over him. After all, he is his boss. Steve doesn't want to risk losing the job in which he has invested so much of his life and himself. In addition, Steve's self-esteem is over-invested in his work, making him feel all the more vulnerable right now. He clearly has a lot at stake both professionally and personally.

• **Hurt** is gnawing away at him too, because a good deal of the content and manner of Dave's attacks is fundamentally unjust. There is no question that Steve is good at his job and his award-winning track record reflects that fact. Sometimes Dave attacks him head on and **explodes** angrily in his face, while on other occasions he **snipes** at him from behind cover, taking advantage of his superior position – or worse still – when in a group. Yet, at the back of his mind, Steve knows that there is some truth in what Dave is saying about his drinking and his recent attitude towards his female colleagues. Cleverly, but unfairly, Dave is working and twisting this grain of truth, forging it into a weapon to use against him. Steve's struggling to get his head around the situation, both on a rational thinking level and emotionally. And this is making it doubly confusing and painful for him.

• **Rage** is also bubbling away underneath all these other emotions. Anger is a natural human response to being attacked and the urge to react aggressively in defence is strong. But Steve dare not let his anger show – at least on the surface – for fear of the consequences. It's an agonizing dilemma for him to be in. And Steve is in inner torment.

The inner bully

Bullies come in all shapes and sizes. The worst bully in your life may even be yourself!

Some are easy to identify such as managers at work, like Dave the Bulldog or colleagues. Others are less obvious, such as Lynn's demanding friends.

Bullies can be in our past, like school bullies, perhaps even some of our teachers.

Steve was bullied at school for being a 'swot'.

But bullies can be closer to home, too. Or, worse still, even *in our home.*

Bullying of all kinds occurs in many families and in this setting can be very destructive and difficult to deal with when you are on the receiving end.

After all, how can you escape from it?

And who do you complain to or confide in?

Family members often bully one another.

It can be partner-to-partner or parent-to-child or between brothers and sisters.

Living side-by-side with the destructive force of bullying erodes self-esteem and slowly destroys self-confidence.

Steve clearly remembers his father bullying him. Those jibes about his school grades, the sarcastic remarks, the embarrassing touchline criticism.

Even now, as an adult, he hears his father's 'voice' inside his own mind, criticizing him and running him down: '... not the sharpest knife in the drawer!'

It's as if Steve's brain recorded and edited these comments and experiences and played back excerpts and snippets from them in the back of his mind throughout the day.

But Steve's grown accustomed to this *inner monologue* because it's happening on the *edge of his awareness.*

He's unfortunately come to accept his *inner critic* as being *normal.*

For some people this inner 'voice' is so clear and distinct and even so loud that they give it a name: my *'**green goblin**'* or my *'**black abbot**'* are common descriptions.

And Steve's inner critic just won't leave him alone!

This experience of a critical inner voice or thoughts is, for Steve, a persistent background noise. It's constantly running him down, questioning his decisions and undermining his self-confidence.

Steve's inner critic has become his own internal bully.

In that sense, he's become his own worst enemy.

To make matters worse, Dave also reminds him of his father. At times, his voice appears to sound just like him.

Steve can sometimes feel like that little boy again, being chastised by his dad.

Steve's **inner bully** and Dave, his **external bully**, are working together to gang up on him!

This adds more power to what Dave is saying and serves to intensify the experience for Steve. No wonder he is taking it all so badly!

Steve is now really having a hard time.

— — — — ▪

Lynn shouted that she was off to see her mother with some shopping – that she'd be back in an hour – and could he switch on the oven in half an hour?

'Right,' said Steve in a uninterested manner.

'Some chance of her being back in an hour!' he thought.

He returned to the lounge to find Nicky playing with his PlayStation.

'Look, Nicky, I told you to clear up this mess before supper. Are you stupid?' he snarled.

Nicky ignored him.

'Well, are you?' demanded Steve. 'Honestly, you're not the sharpest ...' He froze on the last syllable.

Steve quickly brought his right hand to his mouth, as if to stop the words coming out. But it was too late. He had started to say it. Just as his father had said it to him so many times over the years.

A look of horror crossed Steve's face, followed by the saddest of expressions.

Chapter 5

Who are you pruning back to promote healthy growth?

— — — — ▪

Sunday 30 October, 10.45 a.m.

It made a change for Nicky to sleep late and leave Steve and Lynn alone to grab some unexpected extra shut-eye.

The Sunday papers were already scattered across the hallway, after Lynn's earlier foraging, when Steve went to pick up the sports section of the Sunday Times.

'United in Crisis!' screamed the headline, telling him what he knew already.

Determined not to be depressed on this sunny Sunday, he tossed it aside and sank into an armchair with the gardening supplement.

'Prune back now to promote healthy growth!' he read aloud.

'There you are, Lynn. That's what we need to do this afternoon. The front garden's not been touched since the summer.'

'I thought we were taking Nicky to the park before popping in to see mum,' countered Lynn.

'We can do all of that if we just get a move on,' replied Steve.

'I fancy trying this new banana-based diet,' said Lynn, flicking through the celebrity pages. 'Karina from Big Brother was on it and lost a stone and a half.'

'And how long before she put it on again?' asked Steve.

'Doesn't say,' replied Lynn.

'I keep saying it,' began Steve, 'it's not a diet you need, it's ...'

'... exercise', finished Lynn. 'I know, I know. But where ...'

'... would I find the time?' finished Steve. 'Well, if you spent a little less time with your mum and the Three Witches ...'

'Now wait a minute,' replied Lynn, 'we're seeing my mum this afternoon so I don't have to pop in twice in the rush hour this week.'

'Which is great,' replied Steve. 'Now for the Witches ...'

Half an hour later, Steve and Lynn were busy with the first of their commitments – tackling the overgrown and sad-looking front garden of their ground-floor flat.

A bleep came from the mobile in Lynn's fleece, indicating she had a message.

> Who are you pruning back to promote healthy growth?

'Steve, look at this,' said Lynn anxiously. 'I thought these hoax messages had stopped.'

Steve took the mobile and pressed reply, without success.

'I've checked the phone bills,' he began, 'and there's not a trace of them there. So it's not one of these scams. And they still won't delete.'

'You have to admit, Steve – even an old cynic like you – they are very timely. I mean: Who are you pruning back to promote healthy growth? When we're gardening?'

'Yeah, but "who are you pruning?" hardly makes sense,' began Steve.

He emptied more deadheads from the summer's roses into a black bin bag and stopped to address Lynn.

'Although,' he began, 'there are parallels with your life in this garden, Lynn.'

'How do you mean?' enquired Lynn.

'Well, take this heather,' began Steve. 'We planted it here when we moved in four years ago – and look how it's taken over. A bit like Helena. Give her an inch and she takes a mile, without any regard for the other plants – or friends – she's suffocating.'

'So the heather is Helena,' mocked Lynn, hands on hips.

'Well, poisonous ivy would be more appropriate,' taunted Steve, 'but in the absence of any, heather will do.'

Taking his pruners in one hand and a thick stalk of heather in another, Steve cut right through and tossed a large bush of heather in the bin bag.

'And think yourself lucky, Helena,' he threatened, looking at the considerably smaller bush. 'We could have been tougher!'

'Next, let's find Andrea,' he announced, setting his eyes on a soggy, frost-bitten geranium.

'You should have been uprooted years ago, when your friendship with Lynn stopped blossoming and started rotting. You simply have to go!'

As he yanked the dead plant out by the roots, there was little resistance.

Lynn laughed. This was Steve at his best.

'Who's next?' he demanded. 'Where's Clare?'

'Hold on a minute,' intervened Lynn. 'If this garden's our life, let's get some of your deadwood buddies – like Jim,' she said, poised over a rosebush. 'He only ever phones when he wants to come round and watch a match on Sky. How often have you been in his house recently?'

'Fair point,' said Steve. 'Cut him back!'

Her pruners sank into the rose stem, leaving just a few inches above ground.

'A bit severe,' suggested Steve, feigning hurt.

'It'll do him good,' replied Lynn, who continued, 'Now to Bob.'

'Nothing wrong with Bob,' defended Steve.

'As long as you're on the crest of a wave,' continued Lynn. 'Sure, he was all over you like a rash when you were Sales Director of the Year. But where's he been the last six months?'

'Well, the Bulldog's been barking at him too, Lynn,' replied Steve.

'Come on, Steve. These two are buddies. In fact, Bob's always best buddies with whoever's on the crest of a wave. Surely you've noticed that!'

Steve stopped to consider the point. Lynn was absolutely right. Bob always wanted to hang around with whoever was in the spotlight. But he was never there when things got tough.

'Weed him out!' demanded Steve. Lynn uprooted a withered clematis.

'This has been dead for ages,' said Lynn.

'Precisely!' confirmed Steve.

It was his turn now.

'Ladies and gentlemen of the jury, I now present the case for removing Ian and Irene from our lives,' he suggested, grabbing two spent gladioli by the base of the stem.

'But we've known them for years,' pleaded Lynn. 'You can't just throw them out!'

'Yes, we have known them for years,' continued Steve. 'Invited them to our parties, looked after their dog, lent them our car, invited him to the United matches when I've been given tickets. And what have they given us back?'

Lynn paused. 'You can't just bin them, Steve.'

'Watch me,' he threatened.

'No, move them to a corner of the garden,' suggested Lynn, 'and give them a chance to grow next season. We'll just not be staring out the window at them every day.'

In less than an hour, Steve and Lynn had thinned out their plants, disposed of the rotting foliage and were sitting on the doorstep with a coffee, taking in the new appearance of their neat front garden.

'So, Andrea and Bob have gone,' he summarized. 'And Helena and Jim have been pruned severely.'

'And Ian and Irene have a less prominent role, but with a chance to grow,' concluded Lynn.

'Now for the difficult bit,' began Steve. 'The house plants!'

'What house plants?' enquired Lynn.

'I have dastardly plans for the mother-in-law's tongue,' dared Steve, jumping out the way of a friendly swipe from Lynn.

— — — — ▪

The life garden

Steve is beginning to realize that he and Lynn are gradually handing over control of their lives to external factors and to other people.

Too much of Lynn's self-esteem is still invested in pleasing others and Steve's is heavily football-based.

For Steve, his Sunday would have been made if his team had won. Right now he feels depressed.

The defeat of his team is a downer for him.

Lynn, on the other hand – being constantly battered by messages from advertising, TV, magazines and newspapers, urging her to be slim – is upbeat at the thought of a possible new diet. Even though she doesn't really care for bananas.

Lynn and Steve's confidence is up and down, tossed about by the uncertainties of outside events – like celebrity diets and football results.

Factors that are too superficial, too fragile and way too changeable.

Steve and Lynn's self-confidence is at the mercy of outside events rather than being solidly based on an inner sense of personal value.

No wonder they find their mood and self-confidence swinging so wildly!

Granted, this way, Steve feels that life has a sort of a 'buzz'.

But for Lynn it feels fragile, out of her control and a little scary.

And life, by its very nature, brings all sorts of changes that are way beyond their control anyway – so why deliberately add to it?

Steve is perhaps starting to recognize that they are no longer in charge of their lives. Dieting, football and other people have taken over.

He sees that Lynn, by basing too much of her self-confidence on her weight and shape, is only adding to her unhappiness.

Healthy friendships

Steve is more aware that other people, including their friends, have too much control and influence over their lives.

As Lynn and Steve begin to survey their '*life garden*,' he recognizes that Helena is one friend who has become too demanding of Lynn and is choking her life – like an overgrown heather.

He feels that she has been given too much 'space' in Lynn's week and overall takes up way too much of her time.

As a result, other good friends are being 'suffocated' and squeezed out.

Some friends who demand too much time and space need to be 'trimmed' or pruned back.

Another of Lynn's girlfriends, Andrea the 'geranium', was once a good friend to Lynn. He suggests to Lynn that this once-healthy and positive friendship has slowly turned negative, even poisonous.

Andrea has become damaging to Lynn's self-confidence and urgently needs to be rooted out altogether.

Some friends who undermine our self-confidence need to be 'rooted out' completely.

Lynn, on the other hand, equally recognizes that Steve's old buddies Jim and Bob are taking out much more than they give back.

These friendships are no longer mutual and balanced.

She encourages Steve to redress the imbalance in his friendships with Bob and Jim but stops short of removing them completely.

The joint friends of Steve and Lynn, Ian and Irene, the 'gladioli', are a different matter. Once in a very healthy relationship with Lynn and Steve, they have become increasingly exploitative of them over the years.

Perhaps they have simply come to take Lynn and Steve for granted.

Whatever the reason, Steve is tempted to over-react and to root them out altogether.

Lynn feels that they need to be relocated to a different section of their 'life garden' and to be set some new boundaries.

The amount of *time* they spend with them, the **space** that they occupy and the **context** within which they socialize with them could put the relationship back on the right track. In this way, she senses that their friendship with Irene and Ian may be regenerated and perhaps flourish once again.

Some friendships need to be given a chance to grow in a different area of our lives.

Steve and Lynn are gradually understanding that the health of their friendships is affecting their self-confidence and happiness.

— — — — ▇

Driving back from Lynn's mum's house, Steve took an unexpected turning.

'Where are you going?' asked Lynn.

'We're going to the sports centre,' replied Steve.

'Steve, I need to get Nicky to bed, he's tired.'

'We'll be 15 minutes,' replied Steve. 'Because you're going to join for yoga and tennis – and I'm going to join for five-a-side football. And don't dare ask where you'll find the time! Because, if you're going to stick to taking your mum shopping on a Sunday and you're serious about uprooting Andrea and pruning Helena, you've just saved hours each week.'

'OK,' was the unexpected reply from Lynn. 'But don't come running to me in six months bleating about a waste of membership fees.'

'It's a deal,' said Steve, 'if you don't come whining about piling on the pounds because you've stopped going to classes.'

'Done!' said Lynn.

'You certainly have been,' replied Steve.

Chapter 6

Have you lost your bearings?

Monday 21 November, 5.15 p.m.

Being Sales Director of the Year had brought Steve significant perks.

The 5-series BMW was certainly the greatest to someone who had been car-crazy all his life.

But it was more than just a love of cars. Steve liked driving fast. How he had only six points on his licence was a minor miracle.

The Mondeo just didn't feel as good to drive. More to the point, Steve hated the idea of everybody – his clients and his colleagues – knowing that the BMW had gone. It felt like demotion.

For the most part, the holiday in Disneyworld had been great. Even though Nicky had been only four, he'd had a ball. Steve took him on Pirates of the Caribbean, the Peter Pan Ride, It's a Small World. They were like a couple of kids together.

Lynn had thought so also. At times, she'd felt she had two children to keep in order – constantly reminding both to put their baseball caps on in the 90-degree heat and keep topping up the sun cream on exposed limbs.

But when Steve wasn't carrying on with Nicky, he'd taken in the landscape around him – with all the shapes and colours of a gaudy birthday cake – and felt a bit of a fraud. He could barely believe he'd won the trip as reward for his sales efforts. Part of him expected to be 'found out' any minute.

He constantly asked himself if he could have done a bit better and won the two-week cruise round the Caribbean. And he wondered how it would feel next year if they had to return to Majorca instead of Florida.

'Better not get too used to this lifestyle, Lynn,' he'd said more than once.

— — — ▬ ▓

Feeling a fraud

Steve's self-esteem is based on his car, football team, charm and work.

There is no doubt in everyone else's eyes that he is genuinely good at his job.

He won the Sales Director of the Year Award hands down and the company rewarded the Clark family with the trip to Disneyworld.

Yet surprisingly, Steve himself doubts his own worth at work and his personal value to the company. Why?

Because deep down inside Steve feels poorly about himself.

He judges himself too harshly and nothing he achieves is ever good enough for him.

Healthy self-esteem is based on a good inner sense of self-competence (our ability to cope with the challenges of life) – **and** on a
high sense of self-worth (our feeling of value and significance).

Although Steve's self-competence at work is clearly not in doubt,
his evaluation of his own worth is poor.

This is a personal belief he maintains **even though** others hold him
in high regard and would not agree with his poor opinion of himself – if they were aware of it.

Secretly, Steve feels a fraud.

He's constantly trying to prove himself to **himself** and never quite
manages to achieve it.

The pleasure he derived from winning the Regional Sales Director
of the Year Award was short-lived and the brief boost to his low
self-worth faded fast.

This poor sense of self-worth is a painful inner secret that Steve
hides well from his colleagues and friends, even from Lynn.

As a result, he feels like an **impostor** and lives in constant fear of
being **'found out'**.

——— ▪

*Today his worst fears were being realized as the picture of Steve
Clark – Regional Sales Director of the Year – was removed from all
10 divisions, to be replaced by the image of Jim McKenzie. 'Never
thought I'd be usurped by McKenzie,' thought Steve, watching
the office handyman ceremoniously remove his picture. 'He just
seems to get all the breaks.'*

The way things were going, he wondered if it was just his picture that would be replaced.

His dad had always warned him not to get 'ahead' of himself – whatever that meant.

'Maybe he was just trying to protect me from moments like this,' Steve considered.

Steve's daydream was broken by the Bulldog barking, 'Steve, a word in my office.'

He was about to sit down opposite Dave when he was asked to close the door behind him. And this from the man who told the staff every morning, 'My door's always open.'

'Here are your sales figures for the last quarter,' the Bulldog began. 'We both know they're unacceptable, but only one of us has to make decisions about how we deal with them.'

Steve's gaze shot from the chart in front of them to look Dave in the eye. But Dave continued to stare at the piece of paper he was holding.

'We're rewarded on results in this company,' Dave continued. 'But equally, we have to live with the consequences of poor performance.'

'Now wait a minute,' Steve began, 'you can't blame me entirely for what's happened recently.'

'And who else should I blame?' barked back the Bulldog.

Steve hesitated.

'Well?' insisted Dave.

Yet again, Steve faced a dilemma. If he argued, Dave would go for the jugular. If he agreed, he would face whatever fate his boss had in mind, unchallenged.

'I don't think you're being very supportive, Dave,' Steve retorted.

'What do you mean by that?' snarled the Bulldog.

'Well, I could do with some encouragement, rather than the constant sniping,' Steve continued, a little too angrily.

The Bulldog's face reddened. The slight hesitation suggested a large explosion was imminent.

'I wasn't aware it was my job to change your nappies as well as pay your over-inflated salary,' erupted Dave. 'Get a grip and stop being so pathetic. There's a queue of people lining up for your job in this company alone – never mind the dozens of letters of application I receive each month. Now shape up – or ship out!'

Steve glared at Dave, snatched his briefcase and slammed the door on the way out.

He was standing at the bar of the Jug and Claret 20 minutes later, on a second pint. His whisky chaser was finished, so he ordered another.

The barmaid made some pleasant chit-chat but tired of Steve's curt replies and so left him alone.

The latest episode with the Bulldog still bouncing around in his head, Steve left his collection of four empty glasses behind as he strode back to the car park.

Sitting behind the wheel of the Mondeo, waiting to pull out on to the busy road, he stared at the factory wall in the industrial estate across from the pub.

He considered what speed he could reach if he were to drive straight into it: 50 or 60 miles an hour perhaps?

Would that be enough to kill him, or just leave him badly injured?

Lynn and Nicky would be all right, he concluded. He was well insured.

He might feel nothing – yet all his problems would be over.

Steve started to rev the engine, sending clouds of exhaust fumes across the car park.

He gripped the wheel tightly and pressed the accelerator to the floor, screeching out towards the wall.

He swung the car round violently into the flow of traffic, as an image of Nicky flashed across his mind.

━ ━ ━ ▄ ▓

Coping

Given Steve's poor sense of self-worth, it's no wonder that Dave the Bulldog's criticism cuts deeply and feels so painful.

Lynn knows he's hurting but, because she is unaware of just how poorly Steve really views himself, she has no idea how badly he's taking it all and how close he is to 'cracking up'.

Steve feels as if he can no longer cope with it all and, like many men in similar situations of extreme stress, he firstly:

'bottles it up'
and then
'takes to the bottle'.

Men find it more difficult to talk about their worries than women – to express how they feel and to share what they are going through with others, often for fear of being seen as 'weak'.

They can turn inwards on themselves and find temporary relief from drinking alcohol to excess.

Sometimes they feel like harming themselves and may even consider ending it all. And Steve is no exception. He takes to the pub and consumes more beer and spirits than usual. His suppressed rage at Bulldog Dave is boiling away inside and he begins to turn his anger inwards against himself.

Steve starts to think about injuring himself – even of killing himself – until the stark consequence of leaving Nicky fatherless stops him.

— — — — ▪

Steve drove erratically for several miles of the usual route home – but his thoughts were elsewhere when his junction came and went.

Taking the next junction and a less familiar road, he found himself in a poorly-lit industrial estate, where each street looked similar to the next.

After several attempts at finding the exit, Steve pulled up beside a large glass-fronted map of the estate in a desperate attempt to find a way out. As he rolled down the window to look, a text lit up his mobile screen:

> Have you lost your bearings?

— — — — ▪

Keeping your bearings in a relationship

Steve is losing his bearings in his relationship with Lynn.

This is reflected by the fact that she often feels as if she has two children to look after instead of one.

Steve has got so caught up in his successful career that he has begun to opt out of his role as a partner to Lynn and as a parent to Nicky. He may not realize he's doing this and is certainly not intending to, but nonetheless it is happening and Lynn senses it.

Steve believes it's **her** job to care for Nicky on a day-to-day basis, even though **both** he and Lynn work full time. To make matters worse he's rarely home early enough during the week to spend much time with Nicky and at weekends his head is taken up with football, rather than family.

And Lynn, for her part, has bought into this behaviour and the belief underlying it, without ever questioning it.

Family holidays often bring issues to the surface and into sharp focus, perhaps because people spend more time together and for longer periods than at any other point in the year.

When on holiday in Disneyworld, Steve avoided adult responsibility, behaving like a kid, and Lynn found herself parenting both him and Nicky – and began to resent it.

Of course, Steve deserved to have a good time and no doubt Nicky enjoyed the fact that his dad was joining in the fun. That's healthy.

However, if Steve spends too much time behaving like a playful child then the relationship between Lynn and Steve may become unbalanced.

The result could be that Lynn begins to view Steve more as *another child* she has responsibility for, rather than as her partner. In other words, as if she were his *'mother'*. And Steve may increasingly find himself behaving towards Lynn as if she were a *mother figure* and less and less like his partner.

All relationships need to be flexible, but the problem here is that the more time Lynn spends parenting Steve, the more likely it is that she may slowly lose respect and desire for him *as her partner*.

And Steve may increasingly look outside their relationship and begin to see *other women* as possible partners the more time he spends in child mode with Lynn.

Relating to each other as equal adult partners *enough of the time* is something that needs to be kept in balance, otherwise any relationship can begin to lose its bearings.

— — — —

Mobile in hand, Steve stood by the fading industrial estate directory. The estate was roughly circular, in four distinct quadrants – with main roads running north–south and east–west.

In the south-east quadrant was a red dot, accompanied by the words YOU ARE HERE.

But, without references beyond the estate's perimeter, Steve had no idea which way would lead him home.

Greenway Industrial Estate Map

YOU
ARE
HERE

Another message was coming in to his phone. But instead of a text, it was a picture of a circle, in quadrants with a dot in the south-east corner.

An arrow was pointing north-east.

Steve held it up to the directory to compare images. His cynicism around these continuing 'coincidences' was put to the test. But in the absence of any better idea, he returned to the car and sped off on a north-easterly route. Within minutes, he rejoined the ring road and was heading home.

'Steve, what on earth's the matter?' urged Lynn as the dishevelled figure walked through the door. 'You never phoned to say you were on your way.'

'I got lost,' he replied, his mind still far away.

'Lost?' questioned Lynn in disbelief. 'Mr 'I-can't-understand-how-you-can't-find-your-way-about-town-in-the-car got lost!'

'For God's sake leave it out, Lynn,' Steve snapped. 'I've had a terrible day and I just got confused.'

'Steve, what's wrong with you?' begged Lynn, now worried by her husband's alien attitude.

'I began to wonder if I could cope with much more of this, Lynn. And I was thinking just how easy it would be just to give up,' he replied, fighting back tears.

Lynn put both arms around his neck and gave him a kiss, before resting her head on his shoulder.

'You can't do that, Steve,' she eventually answered. 'Nicky and I need you to be strong.'

Lynn still hadn't caught the depth of Steve's mood and left their embrace to pour a glass of wine for them both.

As Steve took off his jacket, he caught sight of Lynn's laptop on the desk. Something about the image on the screen was familiar, so he sat down to study it more closely.

It was similar to his picture text – only with words across each axis.

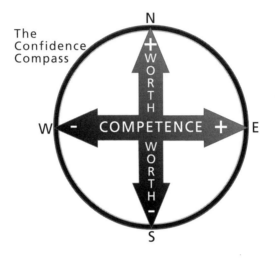

'Lynn, what's this?' he enquired.

'Oh, just something I found on the Internet,' she replied.

'But what is it?' persisted Steve.

'It's a compass that helps you get your confidence bearings,' she replied.

'And what's this arrow pointing north-east?' he probed.

'That's the direction you take to find genuine confidence – based on healthy self-worth and good self-competence,' she answered.

'Apparently all the truly confident people are up in the north-east section.'

'And what about the south-east section?' asked Steve.

'They're "driven",' replied Lynn. 'Often to an early grave!'

— — — — ▩

Modern taboo

Catching sight of the **Confidence Compass** is definitely useful because it immediately *distracts* Steve from his inner state of distress.

Somehow it brings him a sense of *hope* and his thoughts and feelings of self-harm recede from his mind.

Talking about suicide may have replaced talking about sex as a modern day taboo. After all, it's hardly acceptable pub chat! And yet thoughts and feelings of self-harm are experienced by many people at some time in their lives. They are actually just part of the human condition – they come with the territory.

Steve really needs to talk to a good mate, a friend, to someone, even to Lynn herself, but he holds back. It is a pity she doesn't pick up on his desperate mood and ask him about his feelings because *talking helps*.

Chapter 7

Are you heading north-east?

Later that night

Steve stood in the shower for 20 minutes, cleansing away the excesses of his early-evening sorrow-drowning visit to the Jug and Claret.

He played over in his mind the image of the factory wall – and his thoughts of driving into it. But he couldn't contemplate telling Lynn.

He felt such a failure.

'I was at yoga tonight,' volunteered Lynn when Steve re-emerged, hair wet, in his dressing gown.

'Yeah?' replied Steve, making an effort to sound interested.

'It was great,' she continued. 'I dropped Nicky off with mum and had an hour of "me" time. We did all sorts of stretching exercises and deep breathing, followed by a relaxation period at the end when we had to visualize tranquil images.'

Steve was visualizing little else than the pictures running through his mind of brick walls and unfamiliar industrial estates.

'At the end,' persisted Lynn, 'I almost fell asleep. But I could hear the instructor's voice in the background. It was fantastic. Felt as if I'd had a great night's sleep.'

'Great,' said Steve, a little more encouragingly. 'Sounds like you're really enjoying it.'

'So when are you starting five-a-side football?' asked Lynn.

'I can't even think of that right now,' he replied. 'I've got too much on my mind.'

'All the more reason to go and get some exercise,' Lynn replied.

Over supper, the conversation turned to Lynn's earlier description of her husband's attitude to life.

'Lynn, what did you mean when you said I was "driven"?' Steve asked.

'I just meant that you're a man with a mission – always in a hurry – living life at 100 miles an hour – chasing success – but never really enjoying the highs along the way,' came a fuller answer than he had expected.

'But you have to work hard to achieve anything,' replied Steve. 'How can I afford to slow down with the Bulldog chasing me down the garden path?'

'Steve, you've been like that from the moment we met – and probably long before that,' retorted Lynn. 'And when you were flying high last year, you still seemed unable to relax.'

'Well, I always said it would come to an end. I felt I'd be found out,' replied Steve. 'And I was right.'

Steve paused to think before asking, 'So what's the alternative?'

'The alternative is to believe in yourself more,' said Lynn, 'trust your judgement, be aware of your talent, understand that you're good at what you do and focus on success – rather than be terrified of failure.'

'Yeah, but with an overbearing boss …' started Steve.

'It's nothing to do with your boss,' interrupted Lynn. 'You were like that before Dave arrived. It's about you, Steve. Your attitude, your outlook, your self-belief. Just look at this Confidence Compass on my laptop,' she insisted, drawing in a second chair beside the computer.

Lynn brought up the diagram on her screen and started to explain how it worked. Steve's initial resistance became quiet intrigue. He listened to her explanations and began to ask himself deep and searching questions about the way he went about his life.

The Confidence Compass

Steve and Lynn are at a turning point in their lives.

Their awareness of each other's behaviour is about to take a leap forward as they discuss together what makes them tick. This is the first meaningful conversation they've had for some time, since communication between them has recently been strained.

Along with this increased awareness, Lynn and Steve have the wonderful opportunity to change things for the better – to improve the quality of their individual lives as well as their relationship.

There is a genuine opportunity here for them to feel happier about themselves.

There are two axes to the Confidence Compass that Lynn and Steve need to understand if they are to work out their position on it and move in the right direction.

The north–south self-worth axis

Self-worth is to do with having a sense of inner value, significance and goodness – just for being alive rather than for what we do.

It's our own evaluation of ourselves. The further north Steve and Lynn are on the line, the healthier and stronger is their sense of self-worth.

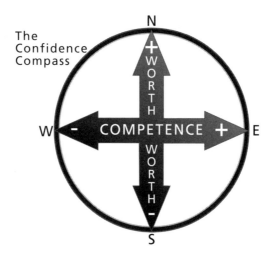

The east–west self-competence axis

Self-competence is about possessing a good set of life skills that are adequate and appropriate to each person's life.

It can vary depending on the situation we are in and upon our circumstances. Clearly, it's possible to possess a good sense of self-competence in one area of our lives, like work for example. But it's also possible to feel like a fish out of water in a different setting, perhaps a social situation such as a party.

It's best summed up as a sense of feeling able to cope with life and its challenges.

The further east Lynn and Steve are on the line, the better their sense of self-competence.

When combined together, healthy self-competence and self-worth bring a sense of being 'good enough' for life.

This is one of the secrets of happiness.

Driven Steve

Steve's learning just how 'driven' he is and how much this has gradually increased over the years without him realizing it.

Lynn is only too quick to point this out and gives him invaluable feedback into the extent of his 'driven-ness' and the effect it has had on those around him, particularly Nicky and her.

Being so focused on achievement in this way is a characteristic of *'south-easterners'* – those who are in the south-east quadrant of the Confidence Compass.

South-easterners are frequently very talented and can often become workaholics.

But their levels of competence and self-worth are unbalanced.

Steve rates himself as a south-easterner. His self-competence is high but his self-worth is low.

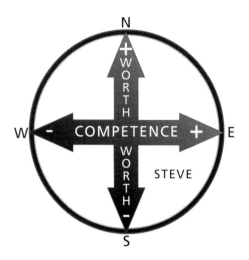

He recognizes that he drives himself on to greater and greater achievements in an attempt to discover a better sense of self-worth – to feel good about himself and his success, deep down inside.

Until now, Steve has had little insight into this aspect of his over-achieving behaviour and has often found himself being excessively self-critical.

Whenever a project is successfully completed, he moves on quickly to the next one, unconsciously hoping that its completion will bring a more lasting sense of self-worth with it.

But somehow it never ever does.

— — — —

'So where are you on this compass?' Steve asked.

'Me?' replied Lynn. 'Well, I'd never really thought …'

'Yes you have,' he shot back. 'Where are you?'

Lynn giggled. She had thought about it for some time, but found it difficult to evaluate her life the way she seemed so comfortable evaluating others'.

'Well, let me look at these sectors one by one,' teased Steve, 'and we'll soon find out where you're hiding. North-west,' he began. 'If I understand what you're saying, this would be someone who's arrogant, through a self-belief that outstrips their ability.'

Lynn looked at him, daring him to attach that label.

'Definitely not!' he concluded. 'No – that would apply to the Bulldog, though. A bully and an arrogant sod.'

'And it would apply to Helena,' volunteered Lynn. 'She's good at spreading tittle-tattle and dwelling on herself, rather than me. Domineering in her behaviour too. Definitely a north-western-er.'

'OK,' began Steve, 'if you're not inhabiting the north-west, are you in the south-east with me? Good at what you do, but unable to believe it – and so driven to success?'

'Certainly not,' asserted Lynn. 'You may feel you have to win everything, but I take a far more pragmatic view.'

'That's just because you hate competition, Lynn,' replied Steve.

'No, I like competition,' explained Lynn. 'So when I play tennis, I play to win. But I don't feel unworthy if I lose.'

'You've lost me,' said Steve, without a hint of irony.

'There's a big difference between wanting to win and feeling you have to beat the opposition to feel better about yourself,' clarified Lynn. 'That's the difference between you and me.'

'Or maybe you're just not all that good at what you do – so you lack competence,' prodded Steve. 'That's perhaps why you're not beside me in the south-east sector.'

'Well, I feel I have a lot to learn at work yet,' began Lynn. 'But it's not just about work. It's about your ability to foster relationships, for a start. And there I think I'm better than you!'

'Oh, so you are *competitive,' teased Steve. 'But not in the south-east! What, then, about the north-east? Are you the rounded, confident person this compass says you'd be if you were up in that quadrant? In fact, does this person exist?'*

'Yes, well, what about your old boss Craig?' suggested Lynn. 'He seemed so comfortable with himself, yet good at motivating others.'

'Correct,' continued Steve. 'And do you know – I once told him that I'd never heard him criticize anybody. He told me that he only ever told people one-to-one what he thought they could do to improve.'

'And yet he's also competitive,' offered Lynn, 'but in a positive way. He got promotion last year, didn't he?'

'Sure, he's the Group Chief Executive now,' finished Steve. 'And, interestingly, he's got there without standing on anybody's neck to climb to the top.'

'You always said you can be too confident, didn't you, Steve?' asked Lynn. 'But Craig's an example of someone who seems genuinely confident, yet a delight to be around.'

A short silence was broken by Steve concluding, 'So, anyway, Craig is a north-easterner – but you're not!'

'Not yet,' began Lynn. 'But that's where I want to be. I think I'm just into the south-west sector and no more, because I'm learn-

ing new skills all the time but I really don't believe enough in myself.'

'You spend too much time pleasing other people and not enough time on yourself,' said Steve.

'But that's changing,' began Lynn, a little impatiently. 'I mean, if you look at what I've done recently – my visits to mum's I've restricted to weekends, where possible – unless I'm dropping Nicky off to let me get to yoga. Also, I've put Helena and Clare off from dropping round recently and instead got the three of us to go out for a meal. And we actually … wait for it … talked about me for a change!'

'Quite right,' continued Steve. 'And you've done all that by being more assertive with your mum and your friends. I reckon that comes from having a bit more belief in your right to make arrangements that suit you instead of everybody else.'

'And I've stopped answering the phone when I'm having dinner,' beamed Lynn.

'It's a request …' began Steve '… not a demand,' finished Lynn.

People pleaser Lynn

Lynn is uncomfortable just thinking about herself, and even more so talking about herself, because she is so used to considering others first. It makes her feel embarrassed, even a little guilty.

Steve provokes her with irritating suggestions about where she is on the self-esteem compass in order to help her overcome her discomfort at talking about herself.

And it works.

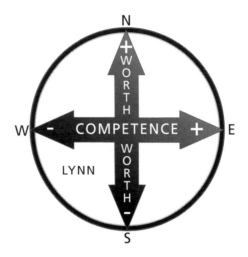

Lynn recognizes that she is in the south-west quadrant – a *'south-westerner.'* Both her sense of self-competence and her self-worth are a little on the low side.

But Lynn also realizes that possessing a good set of life skills is more than just being competent in a work situation. It's also about having good relationship, parenting and friendship skills.

Lynn senses that 'coping' means so much more than just managing well at work.

Coping is about having a range of life skills of a breadth and depth sufficient for life itself.

And Lynn clearly *wants* to change – to improve her coping abilities and to build on her self-worth.

Lynn is planning a quadrant move into the north-east sector. She wants to become a *north-easterner.*

Dave the Bulldog

Some people have very limited abilities in many areas of their lives but think that they're wonderful.

Their self-competence is poor but their sense of self-worth is unrealistically high. They are arrogant, conceited, egocentric and full of grandiose self-beliefs. In other words, they are '*bigheads*'.

And everyone around them knows – but them.

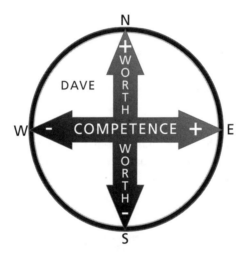

Dave the Bulldog is one of these – a bighead and a bully, too. He thinks inappropriately highly of himself, but others only too clearly see his limitations.

In a sense, he's out of touch with reality about himself while others can see through him only too well.

All bluff and bluster, he most certainly fails to 'walk the talk'.

Dave's speeches sound convincing but his promises are shallow – and seldom translate into appropriate action.

He's an *'emperor with no clothes'* who elects to give himself pompous job titles. Dave exudes a sense of *false confidence*.

This is the type of confidence that is often confused for genuine confidence – masquerading as the real thing.

We often mistake the antics of showmanship for confidence. But authentic confidence produces statesman-like leadership, with integrity.

Confident Craig

Steve's old boss, Craig, is set on the right Confidence Compass setting.

Both Lynn and Steve recognize that Craig possesses a healthy sense of self-worth, which is balanced by a good sense of self-competence that is reality based.

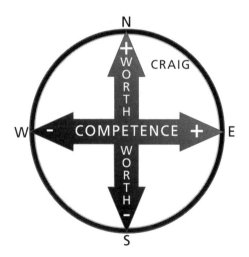

He is confident without being arrogant and successful without being ruthlessly ambitious.

Craig helps others to grow along **with** him because he has nothing invested in **walking over** them in order to get to the top.

Steve and Lynn realize for the first time just what it is that makes Craig such an attractive person, a good colleague and great company.

Craig has good self-esteem and possesses genuine self-confidence.

— — — — ■

'What about you, Steve?' Lynn asked. 'How are you going to head north-east?'

'Well,' Steve began tentatively, 'I suppose I'll have to start believing more in myself. But it's not easy when you hear your dad's voice criticizing you at every turn.'

'He's been dead for years, Steve. And you know his criticism was unfair,' said Lynn. 'Listen instead to what Craig told you – and what I tell you all the time. Surely we know the grown-up Steve much better than your dad ever did!'

'You're right, Lynn. It's just hard,' reflected Steve.

'Well, I'll help you if you help me,' offered Lynn.

'Absolutely,' confirmed Steve. 'Now come to bed and we'll continue this conversation in the morning.'

'Is that a request or a demand?' asked Lynn.

'Both,' laughed Steve.

— — — — ■

Chapter 8

who are your role models?

▬ ▬ ▬ ▬ ▰

Sunday 27 November, 3.30 p.m.

Lynn's mum was delighted to see her daughter and her only grandson.

Doreen Peterson was small and rather frail for her years; a bit too gaunt for Lynn's liking and much too highly-strung.

She gave Lynn a warm hug and threw her arms wide open as she stooped down to welcome Nicky.

'How's the best grandson in the world?' she asked, as he put his arms round her neck.

Fifteen minutes later, the three of them were in Asda – Lynn browsing through the magazines, her mum selecting some sweets with Nicky.

Lynn's mobile indicated that a message had arrived. She pulled it from her bag to read the screen:

who are your role models?

She didn't have to check the sender. It was clearly another in the series they had received for some months.

'Role models?' she considered. 'I don't have any role models.'

Replacing the phone, she continued to scan the magazines filling the extensive shelves in front of her.

The faces before her were familiar, rather like old friends. Elle Macpherson, Claudia Schiffer and Cindy Crawford adorning the covers of Cosmo, Glamour *and* Hello!

Elsewhere Brooke Shields was reflecting on her naked film role when 12 and Halle Berry was discussing the impact of her father Jerome walking out when she was four.

Lynn's mind jumped to the last time she saw her own father. He had left the family when she was 13, but, by that time, Lynn had learned to ignore virtually everything he told her.

If she asked him to come to her dancing show, he would say he'd 'try' – but never turn up.

If she asked if they could go to the cinema, he'd say, 'We'll see' – but they seldom went.

If she asked for some new jeans, he'd say, 'Perhaps' – but they failed to materialize.

Her mother had been the opposite. Doreen Peterson spent her life running after Lynn, and everybody else for that matter. She couldn't do enough for young Lynn. But her dad, whose attention she craved, wouldn't do anything at all.

Over a coffee in the supermarket restaurant, Lynn asked her mother a surprisingly direct question.

'Mum, why did you put up with dad for so long?'

Doreen looked startled, then a little defensive.

'What on earth do you mean by that, Lynn?' she asked back.

'Why did you put up with his lies and letdowns for so many years?' came the equally blunt follow-up question.

'Well we had you to think about,' she began. 'And in those days, couples stayed together for the sake of their children, rather than just splitting up when it suited them.'

'Dad didn't see it that way,' replied Lynn. 'He left just the minute it suited him. Hardly a good role model.' The last phrase slipped out unintentionally.

'Well he was a better role model than any of these celebrities in those magazines you're so fond of,' hit back her mother, rather annoyed at Lynn's tone.

'I don't pay any attention to them,' said Lynn. 'I trust myself to make up my own mind about things.'

'No you don't,' persisted her mum. 'You follow their diets, their beauty tips. You constantly complain that you're overweight, when you're comparing yourself to people who're unnaturally thin.'

Nicky was bored with the bickering and was starting to balance his empty glass on top of the coffee pot.

'Nicky, put that down,' snapped Lynn, who then turned back to her mother. 'Mum, I am overweight and you should be pleased that I diet to keep fit.'

'I'm pleased that you're keeping fit with yoga,' replied Doreen, 'but that's quite different from trying to compete with the body of a 25-year-old supermodel who hasn't had children.'

'Nicky, please put that down at once,' interrupted Lynn.

'Anyway,' continued her mum. 'I didn't come out here for an argument. I ...'

She was cut off mid-sentence by the sound of Nicky's glass smashing into a hundred pieces on the tiled floor.

'Oh, Nicky, I told you not to do that,' shouted Lynn. 'Now look what you've done!'

The restaurant fell quiet. Lynn could feel several pairs of eyes burning into her back.

The two women started picking up pieces of the widely scattered glass, continuing their spat.

'Well, shouting at him in a crowded coffee shop is hardly being a good role model, is it?' prodded Doreen.

'He just ignores me unless I shout,' fired back Lynn.

'He was ignoring you well before you started to shout,' came the blunt and factually correct reply.

— — — — ▓

Choosing healthy role models

Throughout the course of their lives, Lynn and Steve have each acquired a unique set of role models.

These are people they have unconsciously come to look up to for guidance about how to function in society and for direction about how to live life in the complex modern world.

For most of us, our role models are made up of a collection of key figures from our past and present experience, such as parents, family members, schoolteachers, friends and religious figures, through to modern day political leaders, celebrities and stars from the world of music, TV, film and sport.

If Lynn and Steve want to experience genuine self-confidence and a deeper sense of personal happiness it's essential that they adopt *healthy* role models for their lives rather than the most *popular* or the most *obvious* or simply the most *available* ones.

Why? Because healthy role models will help direct Steve and Lynn towards a set of personal beliefs, patterns of behaviour and a style of living that will be life affirming.

Both Lynn and Steve are feeling very insecure right now, as if they have lost their way a little in the maze of life. A poor choice of role models is leading them up some blind alleys.

Unthinkingly following unhelpful role models is contributing to their confusion and increasing their sense that life has currently lost some of its meaning and direction.

Celebrity role models

Lynn, without ever consciously deciding to do so, has at some stage in her past chosen certain celebrities to be among some of her role models. And in doing so she has unwittingly adopted some of their values, beliefs and behaviours.

Relentlessly, on a daily basis, their messages and commands shout out at her from the pages of glossy magazines, and film and TV screens:

Look at ME

YOU ought to look like me, too

You should really be as THIN as I am

Get on this DIET right now

Run your RELATIONSHIPS this way

Live your life like me!

Lynn is surrounded by misleading and pervasive influences. There's no escape. And particularly so because nearly all of her friends share the same beliefs.

Lynn is being brainwashed!

She has bought into these messages and beliefs, telling her how to live life, which scream incessantly at her from the page and screen. But Lynn is forgetting one very important fact: celebrities from the world of fashion, music, TV and film make a living out of creating and promoting an image – *their image*.

And that's the problem. Because an image is misrepresentative of real life and how to live it well. Neither is it based on building real confidence, nor has it necessarily got other people's best interests at heart.

Image promotion is about financial gain rather than about helping others to achieve personal happiness.

Basing her beliefs about her size, shape and weight on the professed views of celebrities is causing Lynn much confusion and dissatisfaction with herself. Even Steve sees it.

After all, when we want to learn to drive we go to a driving instructor – rather than to the Silverstone F1 race track or the dodgems.

Similarly, when we want to learn how to live well, we need to take as models the values, beliefs and behaviour of *genuinely* successful and happy people.

Lynn needs to re-examine her personal beliefs in terms of *whom* and *what* she is basing them on – *to start thinking for herself*.

New role models

To a large extent, children learn by adopting the beliefs, values and behaviour of their parents. They copy them. And we, as adults, continue to use the same process throughout our lives.

Lynn adopted her mother as a key role model from an early age.

She has copied her mother's style of *'meeting everyone else's needs except her own'* and expecting little back, even from her closest family, throughout most of her adult life.

In some ways, Steve reminds Lynn of her father – often absent and emotionally unavailable for much of the time. She sometimes wonders if that's part of what attracted her to Steve in the first place and if it played a part in why she chose and eventually married him.

Steve, as a boy, on the other hand, spent little time with his dad and was bullied by him to some extent in many different and painful ways that gradually eroded his developing sense of self-worth and self-confidence.

Now a parent himself, Steve has learned this pattern of parenting and way of fathering from his dad. But he is now at risk of repeating the same unhelpful and destructive cycle with Nicky. More worryingly, he's unaware that he is doing it.

He's even beginning to bully his female work colleagues.

Like Lynn, Steve too needs to reappraise his behaviour and choice of parental role model. Perhaps he could begin to look to his old boss Craig as a good example of how to relate well to others and achieve a deeper level of personal happiness and success.

Both Lynn and Steve urgently need a new set of role models.

━━ ━━ ━━ ▬ ▇

Steve had prepared a lasagne for Lynn and Nicky's arrival, shortly after five.

As Lynn struggled through her front door, carrying four Asda carrier bags, the smell of food brought about a strange sensation. She felt guilty.

'You didn't have to make supper, Steve. I'd have done that,' she protested.

'Nonsense,' he replied. 'I enjoyed being creative in the kitchen. Well, opening a Marks & Spencer's packet. So, anyway, how was your gran, Nicky?' he enquired.

'She was grumpy,' came Nicky's stark reply.

'Grumpy?' enquired Steve, this time of Lynn. 'Why grumpy?'

'Oh, I don't know,' began Lynn. 'The whole outing was a bit of a disaster. Nicky smashed a glass, Mum was being argumentative …'

'About what?' asked Steve.

'Well, everything,' she replied. 'It started when I asked her why she put up with Dad for so long – continued as she accused me of worshiping celebrities as role models and ended in her questioning my parenting skills. Apart from that, we got on well!'

'She does have a point about the celebs, Lynn,' ventured Steve. 'You do spend an inordinate amount of energy and time following their every fad. And in your mum's day, she would have role models like the Queen, the vicar – and probably the local MP.'

'Well, not many people would regard any of them as role models today,' replied Lynn. 'Head of a dysfunctional family, head of a church that tells you each week how sinful you are – and a man who tells lies for a living!'

'My God, your mother really has rattled your cage!' exclaimed Steve. 'I didn't realize you held these pillars of society in such contempt.'

'Well, I just question who you should listen to these days,' answered Lynn.

'Well, just consider the people you admire, Lynn,' suggested Steve.

'Like?' asked Lynn.

'Like your yoga teacher,' he replied. 'You really respect her.'

'That's true,' said Lynn. 'She's just got a well-rounded personality, I suppose.'

'And you could also listen more to yourself, Lynn,' offered Steve. 'Because from what I see of your bank colleagues, others listen to you.'

Chapter 9

Who are you parenting?

Wednesday 14 December, 8.30 a.m.

Steve felt he could ill-afford the time to see a doctor, especially over such a stupid thing as indigestion.

Lynn had persuaded him, however, that he had had these bouts too long and that he should visit the GP. She'd even made the appointment.

In front of him in the surgery waiting room sat the usual collection of magazines: Woman's Own, New Look, Cosmopolitan, Golf World *and* Hello!

'So, four out of five visitors to the doctor are women,' mused Steve, 'and the only man is a golfer!'

As a non-golfer, he had little interest in picking up the magazine. And while intrigued about the sex survey on the front page of Cosmo, he felt too embarrassed to look at that, either.

Instead, his eyes scanned the walls: advice on bowel cancer, safe sex and parenting skills.

'Well, if you practised safe sex, you wouldn't need to learn parenting skills,' Steve considered, frustrated there was no audience for his humour.

His phone sounded with a message:

> ## who are you parenting?

'Ah, our mystery phone pest,' thought Steve. He scrolled down, but that was the end of the message.

'Well, that's the easiest one so far,' he considered. 'One child. Aged five. Next question.'

'Steven Clark,' announced the receptionist. He approached the counter and was told to see Dr Davidson in room three.

'Morning,' said the doctor. 'What's troubling you?'

'Nothing,' said Steve, 'but my indigestion is troubling my wife.'

For several minutes they exchanged questions and answers on Steve's eating habits, drinking pattern and lifestyle. He underplayed the late-night carry-out food and after-work drinks – and overplayed his occasional game of five-a-side football.

'Are you under a lot of pressure at work?' asked Dr Davidson.

'Goes with the territory,' was Steve's glib reply.

Driving to his first sales call, after leaving the surgery, Steve's mobile rang.

'Well?' enquired a friendly voice.

'Oh, hi, Gorgeous!' Steve replied.

'Well, what did the doctor say?' asked Lynn.

'Oh, he just gave me a prescription to counter stomach acid and suggested I exercise a bit to lose some weight, cheeky bugger!' replied Steve. 'You should see his beer belly!'

'Did you tell him you'd been stressed out of your box at work?' persisted Lynn.

'Yes, we discussed that,' fudged Steve. 'Anyway, I'll take that stuff and that'll sort it.'

'Steve, you are awful when it comes to looking after your health!' continued Lynn.

'Now you're sounding like my mum, Lynn,' replied Steve in mock aggravation.

'Well, seeing she's not speaking to you these days, somebody needs to look after you since you won't do it yourself,' teased Lynn.

'Hey, I got another of these funny messages this morning,' Steve said, changing the subject.

'What this time?' enquired Lynn.

'Who are you parenting?' replied Steve.

'And what do you think the answer is?' asked Lynn.

'Well, Nicky of course,' offered Steve.

'Mmm,' came the surprising response.

'What?' asked Steve, a little hurt – but apprehensive of where this was going.

'I'm saying nothing,' said Lynn.

'Actually, you're saying everything,' said Steve. 'Are you saying I'm not parenting Nicky?'

'Well, you're sometimes there in body, but seldom in spirit,' suggested Lynn.

'That's so unfair, Lynn,' shot back Steve. 'You know I dote on him.'

'I know you do,' replied Lynn. 'But does he know that?'

'Well, if you mean, do I smother him like you do in a you-can-never-do-anything-wrong kind of way, well, no I don't,' hit back Steve, now sounding more than a little irritated.

'Steve, that's so cruel,' protested Lynn. 'Look, we'll talk about this later. I have to go.'

The phone went dead. As Steve drove on, he swallowed hard as his stomach burned. The indigestion was back with a vengeance.

That evening, 8.10 p.m.

Steve walked into the kitchen that night to find Lynn alone, having put Nicky to bed.

'Well, that was charming,' hissed Steve.

'What?' asked Lynn, confused by his opening comment.

'You hung up on me, that's what,' continued Steve.

'No, I didn't,' defended Lynn. 'I had a colleague walk in and I didn't want to share a personal conversation with her. I told you I had to go.'

'Well, you sounded miffed,' continued Steve.

'I was just being honest,' protested Lynn. 'Surely you want that, rather than some insincere palm-off about you being a wonderful father.'

'Oh, I don't know,' began Steve, his mood softening. 'I rather like the sound of that.'

'Look, Steve, I know you're under the cosh at work just now, but Nicky doesn't and I just feel you could do with treating him the way you used to,' said Lynn, '… as if he was the most wonderful child ever created.'

'He knows I love him to bits,' replied Steve.

'When did you last tell him?' asked Lynn.

'I tell him all the time,' offered Steve.

'You used to,' began Lynn. 'But I doubt if I've heard you tell him that in the last two years.'

'Now hold on Lynn,' came back Steve. 'You go overboard to the extent that you can never give Nicky a row.'

'That's not true,' said Lynn.

'But it's so true,' continued Steve. 'I've watched you as you ask him not to do things – he ignores you – then you fail to deal with the consequences. No wonder he plays up with you.'

'You just bark at him,' she replied.

'You just let him run wild,' hit back Steve.

'Well, I'd rather he knew I loved him unconditionally,' replied Lynn.

'Well, I'd rather he knew when he'd overstepped the mark,' came back Steve.

'Steve, you've complained for years about your critical father, but more and more you can only point out what he's doing wrong,' complained Lynn.

'Well, if that's the case, you've become your mother,' replied Steve. 'You'll do anything rather than upset him, so you now have a five-year-old running your life.'

'Steve, what else am I meant to do? You're never home till after eight. You're normally exhausted and I'm being left to bring him up on my own,' protested Lynn, now exasperated by the conversation.

'Well, try doing my job,' suggested Steve, unhelpfully.

'No, try doing my job … and raising a child on your own,' was Lynn's match-winning point.

_ _ _ _ ■

Your parenting style

Parenting is one of the few jobs in life that is acquired without any qualifications.

And yet, arguably, it's the most important job in the world.

The process through which a new personality and the identity of another person is forged and then moulded into shape is the great wonder of parenting.

Lynn's well aware that effective parenting combines the skills and art of both mothering and fathering, in equal amounts. She feels that, when it comes to fathering Nicky, Steve is not pulling his weight and so she reminds him of this truth.

However, to be fair, he has only his *own* experience of being parented as a child to draw on. And that was far from perfect.

Steve's mother did nearly all of his parenting, both the mothering and the fathering.

His dad was an emotionally remote man and overcritical whenever he spoke. He seemed to think it was his job in life to keep little Steven in his place, as it were, to put him down and to keep him there.

A sort of variation on the old theme of *'being seen but not heard'* but, from an emotional perspective, more like *'allowed to exist but not to thrive'*.

Steve's father needed to be 'in charge' or at least to feel that he was. For him, parenting was all about *power*.

Fathering meant discipline, threatening punishment and dishing out his unique acidic form of sarcastic criticism.

Encouragement was definitely not a part of his parenting repertoire and praise was seen as a foreign language that only occasionally Steve's mother was allowed to use.

Steve cannot recall his father ever telling him that he loved him at any time in his life. It is therefore no surprise that he in turn now struggles to tell Nicky he loves him.

As it was in his family of origin, so it is now in Steve's own family. In reality, Lynn does most of the parenting.

And this involves aspects of fathering as well as mothering. Increasingly, Lynn is feeling resentful at being overburdened in this way.

When she raises the issue with Steve, it makes him feel uncomfortable, anxious and even angry. He senses that he's not getting it quite right with Nicky but he has no idea just where he's going wrong or how to fix it.

Lynn, on the other hand, overcompensates for Steve's critical sharpness with Nicky and at times finds herself over-indulging him as a result.

Being a people pleaser like her mother, she cannot bear witnessing Nicky squirm when she occasionally scolds him. At a deeper level, she fears that, if she does, he might end up *disliking her*.

And that would be a significant threat to her already fragile self-worth that she cannot risk.

Healthy parenting practices

Lynn once read that there is a set of healthy principles underlying good parenting. She knows that if she gets these right, *enough of the time*, then Nicky should turn out OK.

She remembers them to be:

Loving the person your child is – unconditionally

Of course, she realizes this means that she does not need to love or necessarily like *all of Nicky's behaviour* – even if she loves *all of him as a person*.

Setting clear, understandable and consistent boundaries to behaviour

Without boundaries, Nicky will be 'all over the place' – both physically and emotionally.

Only when clear boundaries to behaviour are consistently upheld will the outside world appear **rational, predictable** and **safe** to him. Only then will it make 'sense' to him and bring security to his inner world. Always eager to please Nicky, Lynn is aware that she struggles to consistently deliver on this one.

Respecting a child's individuality

Lynn knows that Nicky needs to be allowed to be himself – to develop his own unique personality. But Steve has a need to see Nicky conform to *his* own personal likes and dislikes, just as his dad did with him.

Having high yet realistic expectations

Well, this is a tough one for Steve. He's constantly niggling at Nicky in a negative way, very similar to how his own father behaved – always making him feel that he had somehow fallen short of the mark and was never 'good enough' to win his approval.

High expectations will give Nicky confidence that his parents *believe* in him and therefore help him build real confidence in himself.

Realistic expectations will ensure he avoids being set up to fail. Instead, he's primed for success.

Parenting styles

Lynn and Steve's parenting styles are out of balance:

• Steve is too autocratic and Lynn too permissive.

• Lynn does most of the mothering and the fathering while Steve opts out.

- Lynn is emotionally over-involved with Nicky and meets her own emotional needs through him.

- Steve, on the other hand, is emotionally both under-involved and remote.

Lynn and Steve need to work out their parenting issues together, so that they are talking the same language and are *consistent* in the way they relate to Nicky.

Currently, Lynn says one thing to Nicky – and a moment or two later, Steve *contradicts* it.

More confusing still is the fact that Steve will often clearly express his views on behaviour to Nicky and then do the *opposite* himself.

As a result, *congruence* between what his parents *say* and what they *do* is lost. And as a consequence, so is Nicky!

Self-parenting

Having said that, it comes as no surprise that when Steve develops some stomach symptoms, he's reluctant to go to the GP. Somehow he sees physical illness as a sign of weakness.

In addition, because he was never adequately nurtured and parented as a child himself, he finds it alien to take care of himself in a loving way now, as an adult – in other words to *'parent himself'*.

The skill of self-parenting is one of the secrets of being able to cope with life.

This is both the process and practice of relating to oneself in the way that a good parent would – with love, self-respect, self-acceptance, boundaries to behaviour, care, support, a sense of personal responsibility and with self-encouragement.

Although Lynn and Steve are doing the best they can at the moment, given their own experiences of being parented as children themselves, they need to learn to parent Nicky, themselves and each other in a more balanced and effective way.

As a consequence, the confidence-sapping cycle of unhelpful family parenting can be broken and their family life greatly enriched.

— — — — ▉

The lamb chops were consumed with very few words spoken.

Lynn was upset at the row that had broken out and began, internally, to blame herself for escalating the discussion.

Steve was fuming, wondering how a text question had provoked such a blazing row.

'I'm going to the phone shop tomorrow to find out how to stop these bloody text questions,' he insisted.

'It's not the questions that cause the rows, Steve,' offered Lynn insightfully. 'It's the answers.'

'Either way, I'm fed up with it,' said Steve.

'Well, surely it's good to discuss these things,' said Lynn. 'As long as we're both reasonable about it.'

'Agreed,' admitted Steve, reluctantly.

'OK then,' ventured Lynn, 'if the question was "Who are you parenting?" have you asked yourself who else apart from Nicky that could refer to?'

'Nope,' said Steve, still in an uninterested manner.

'Well, there's your sales staff,' said Lynn.

'They're old enough to look after themselves,' snapped back Steve.

'You said you'd be reasonable,' chastised Lynn.

'OK, OK,' replied Steve. 'And your point is?'

'My point is that you need to be a good "dad" to your staff,' suggested Lynn.

'And love them unconditionally?' he queried.

'No, just respect them unconditionally,' answered Lynn. 'You already set them clear boundaries and targets. And you treat them as individuals. If you showed them a bit more respect, Dave couldn't accuse you of bullying them.'

Steve stopped to consider Lynn's point. He knew she was right.

'And while we're on the subject of parenting,' she continued, 'I sometimes feel you and Nicky are both behaving like kids and I'm the only parent.'

'I feel that when I organize all your paperwork and you don't take responsibility for yourself,' replied Steve. 'And when I point it out, you behave like a disgruntled teenager.'

'And what did you tell me this morning?' came back Lynn. 'You told me I was sounding like your mum because I wanted to know what the doctor told you.'

'Well, maybe we both act as each other's parents at times,' said Steve.

'Perhaps we could both act as adults once in a while then,' suggested Lynn.

'What ... and start acting responsibly?' teased Steve. *'How un-imaginably awful!'*

Chapter 10

How are you coping with change?

━ ━ ━ ▬ ▉

Sunday 1 January, 11.30 a.m.

The roads were quiet as Steve, Lynn and Nicky set out to see Ian and Irene Brown on New Year's Day – as they had done each January 1st for the past 10 years.

'This is the first time in two months I'll have seen Irene,' pointed out Lynn.

'Quite,' observed Steve. 'And how has she taken to being pruned back in our social garden?'

'Well, she did ask a couple of weeks ago if she'd done anything to upset me,' replied Lynn.

'Funnily enough, Ian stopped asking for United tickets when I turned him down three times in a row,' observed Steve.

'And have you missed his company?' asked Lynn.

'Well, no – but, in a funny sort of way, I'm looking forward to catching up today,' he replied.

The Mondeo approached an unfamiliar road junction.

'This is all different since we were here last,' said Lynn.

'Yep, look at the road sign,' added Steve. 'CHANGED PRIORITIES AHEAD. Rather apt, given the conversation, don't you think?'

Lynn's phone bleeped with a new text message:

> How are you coping with change?

'This is weird,' suggested Lynn, reading out the text.

'It's as if someone is playing games with us,' said Steve. 'Watching our every move.'

'So, how are we coping with change, Steve?' asked Lynn.

'Well, what change?' asked Steve. 'Seeing Ian and Irene less often?'

'As a starter, yes,' offered Lynn.

'Well, that's working out for the better,' said Steve. 'And so are the other changes with our friends. I don't particularly detect many noses out of joint.'

'Well, Mum's was at first,' replied Lynn. 'She thought I just didn't want to see her as often. But in fairness, I see her when my time allows – and she's keeping Nicky when I'm at yoga.'

'And on a couple of occasions when I've been playing football,' added Steve.

'What about the changes at work?' asked Lynn.

'Well, that's just been a nightmare since the Bulldog replaced Craig,' said Steve. 'I don't know how anybody is meant to cope with that.'

'Perhaps you need to stand up to him,' suggested Lynn.

'And lose my job?' replied Steve. 'No thanks. Not with a mortgage, wife and child to support.'

'Well, you've made positive changes with your staff,' offered Lynn.

'True,' replied Steve. 'And in fairness, they've responded more positively since I took a more "fatherly" approach this last fortnight. Anyway, enough about me. What about you?'

'What about me?' came Lynn's cautious reply.

'Well, you've had to cope with a huge change since going back to full-time work in September,' prompted Steve.

'Yes, and at the same time seeing Nicky start school and after-school club, which made me feel terribly guilty,' replied Lynn.

'You don't still feel guilty?' asked Steve.

'Sometimes I do,' came her candid reply. 'Especially when I get a phone call to say he's been sick in class, which happened in his second week. Remember?'

'I'd forgotten that,' said Steve.

'Well, I haven't,' replied Lynn. 'It was terrible timing, as I was running my first seminar and was unable to go and pick him up.'

'Oh, I remember,' recalled Steve. 'Your mum went to get him.'

'On two buses,' added Lynn. 'Hence the guilt.'

Having been stuck behind a tractor for the previous three miles, Steve put his foot down to overtake. But the car responded less *quickly than he anticipated and he was forced to abort the manoeuvre.*

'Steve, be careful!' screamed Lynn. 'We're not in the BMW now.'

'And that's another thing,' suggested Steve. 'It's been very difficult going from being Regional Sales Director of the Year – driving a top-of-the-range car – to being an idiot, in Dave's eyes, driving a Ford Mondeo.'

'You're such a car snob,' prodded Lynn. 'I don't care what car you drive.'

'Well I do,' replied Steve.

'So not coping too well with that change, Steve?' teased Lynn.

'Very funny,' replied Steve, unamused. 'Anyway, your job – how are you dealing with it?'

'It's a bit scary,' began Lynn. 'I did feel very vulnerable going back after almost five years away. Everything had changed: the computers, the methods, some of the people. But I have to say, I have felt much better about it the last month or so.'

'More confident?' asked Steve.

'Yes, getting there,' was Lynn's less-than-confident reply.

'So are you a north-easterner yet?' he probed, referring to their positioning on the Confidence Compass.

'As I say, getting there,' said Lynn. 'I do feel as if I'm running after people less and doing a bit more of what I want. And what about you? Have you turned the corner yet?'

'Well, I have played five-a-side a few times recently,' Steve suggested.

'Still rather driven though,' replied Lynn.

'Come on, you can't expect change overnight.'

'No, but this year, Steve,' pushed Lynn, 'you should make that your New Year's Resolution.'

'What – to be less driven?' answered Steve. 'Not much of a resolution that.'

'Well, if you're less driven and more confident, you'll find yourself much happier,' offered Lynn. 'Surely it's OK to resolve to be happier this year?'

'It just sounds so pathetic. "I just want to be happy",' he mocked in a feeble tone. 'Sounds like the kind of thing your mum would say.'

'OK then,' said Lynn, preparing herself for a challenge, 'if you were offered the choice of success at work or happiness, which would you take?'

'Success,' replied Steve in an instant.

'And if you were successful but unhappy, what would that make you?' she continued.

'Successful!' replied Steve triumphantly.

'Successful yet unhappy,' finished Lynn. 'Now, if you were less successful, yet happy, what would that make you?' asked Lynn, anticipating the same obtuse answer.

'Less successful,' came the predictable response.

'Yet *happy,' finished Lynn, exasperated. 'Whichever way you look at it, Steve, if you're happy,* you're happy – *regardless of what life throws at you. And that surely is* real *success.'*

To change or not to change?

Being alive is really all about change.

This is because change is a central dynamic force in life itself.

Being at the core of the very process of living, it is therefore un-avoidable and inescapable.

But how we perceive change, what meaning it holds for us and the way in which we respond to it, is closely connected with how we see ourselves and the world around us.

The extent to which change impacts upon us is related to our level of self-worth and our sense of being able to cope with whatever changes life brings our way.

Predictable change

Steve and Lynn are currently going through a series of significant personal changes and they are occurring at a rate they have never experienced before.

It's all beginning to become a bit scary for them and out of their control.

For some years now, on the surface, their life together has just been ticking along nicely, in the general way that we all tend to expect and hope it will do. A few small glitches here and there, interspersed with the odd significant life event such as the arrival of Nicky, but nothing out of the ordinary run of the mill.

In recent times, the changes that Lynn and Steve have had to deal with have been *predictable* if not actually *planned*.

They could choose *if* they wanted to make a change in their lives and even *when* this would occur.

In other words, the nature and level of change they have experienced to date has largely been under *their own personal control*.

They decided when to have a child together, if Lynn should return to full-time work and, more recently, to see less of their friends Ian and Irene, as well as to set some new clear boundaries in their relationship with Lynn's demanding mother.

Undoubtedly, this kind of predictable and planned change requires some degree of personal adjustment. But most of the time it is relatively straightforward and easy to deal with.

The challenge of unforeseeable change

By its very nature, life is unpredictable – it frequently involves changes over which we have little or no control.

Unexpected and unforeseeable events occur to all of us, whether we like them or not, and Steve and Lynn are no exception.

Steve had no influence over whether his old boss left or stayed with the company and he was devastated when Craig moved on. Until Craig actually left, he had no real idea of the astonishing confidence-building effect his old boss had been having on him.

The dramatic arrival of Dave the Bulldog has been a great blow to Steve and Dave is rapidly becoming a significant thorn in Steve's side.

This, coupled with the replacement of his treasured BMW by the Mondeo, has led to Steve's self-confidence being given a massive knock.

The more our confidence is built on *external* factors over which we have little or no control, like they are with Steve, then the more vulnerable we feel in the face of life's changes.

Confidence is an inner state, rather than a set of circumstances.

The remarkable life of Christopher Reeve (the actor best known for his role as Superman), who was paralysed from the neck down following a horse riding accident, is a remarkable example of this life truth.

How he coped with this tragedy was a reflection of his inner confidence and positive attitude.

In the same way, how well Lynn and Steve cope with the changes happening to them will be dependent to a large extent on the level of their *inner* state of self-confidence.

If this *inner core* of confidence is strong then they will feel less vulnerable to the 'slings and arrows' of ordinary life, because it is less dependent on *external* factors and events over which they have minimal influence.

Fear of change

Fear of change is one of the biggest confidence killers.

Given the choice, most people shy away from it; they prefer things around them to be consistent and to have a feeling of familiarity and sameness about them, since this offers a sense of security.

But there is actually no real security in sameness, since it goes against the flow of life, the essential nature of which is built around the principle of constant change and growth.

The ever-changing, developing and evolving natural world around us provides ample evidence of this fact. Summer becomes autumn, becomes winter, becomes spring … becomes summer. Change is essential for renewal to take place.

The Message of Life is clear:

Adapt

Adjust

Amend

Modify

Develop

Grow

Transform

CHANGE

or

Diminish

Wither

Die

A real sense of security for Steve and Lynn will develop when their confidence is based on a healthy inner sense of self-worth and self-competence.

A *belief* that they **will** cope with the changes that are coming their way, whatever they may be.

Our level of confidence is at the heart of how well we deal with the prospect of change.

—— —— —— ▬▬ ▉

After some 20 minutes in the car, the Mondeo pulled into Ian and Irene Brown's driveway.

Unexpectedly, Ian was standing at the door, looking rather agitated.

'Good God, look at Ian,' said Lynn, sensing something wrong. 'He looks as if he's dreading this visit. Maybe their noses are out of joint.'

Ian stepped over to Steve's car door and started to open it for him.

'Hi, Ian, nice to see you,' began Steve, overcompensating for the atmosphere he sensed.

'Steve, I'm afraid I've got some, some really bad news for you, mate,' Ian began, falteringly.

'What's that?' asked Steve, completely baffled.

'It's your mum. I'm afraid she's passed away.'

Steve's head flooded with emotions:

Shock at news for which he was completely unprepared.

Bewilderment that his friend was telling him about the death of his own mother.

Guilt that it had been two years since he had last spoken to her.

'What happened?' was all that he could manage to utter.

'She died of cancer,' replied Ian. 'My mum just phoned me an hour ago to tell me. They still kept in touch, as you know.'

'Of course,' said Steve, now numb, 'which is more than I did.'

Steve and his mother had had a huge row after his father's funeral seven years earlier, when he had dared to say what he had thought of him.

His mother had initially put the row aside, but refused point blank to speak to Steve after Christmas dinner five years later, when Steve again spoke out loudly against his father, after getting drunk.

He'd gone even further by accusing his mother of standing back and failing to challenge his father's bullying behaviour.

'When did she die?' asked Steve.

'Just yesterday,' came the reply.

Instead of feeling relieved at picking up the news quickly, Steve now knew he would face a dilemma over whether to attend the funeral.

— — — ▬ ▇

Responding to change

The sudden news of his mother's death raises many issues for Steve.

It is a classic example of the way in which the message that life is unpredictable and ever changing can be brought home so starkly.

And there is no greater example of change than the cycle of birth and death itself.

These experiences are part of the human condition and touch us to our core.

Steve is left reeling from the shocking news.

Just how he copes with his grief will be a test of his ability to process his feelings of sadness, denial, loss, anger and guilt that are part of mourning.

Perhaps he will find a way to express his emotions without turning to alcohol and burying himself in his work, which might hinder the healing process.

Grieving cannot be dodged if real recovery is to take place.

But perhaps his mother's death will act as a catalyst for growth and change if Steve can find the courage to explore the personal meanings and emotional messages for him that are contained within this painful experience.

Every life experience, positive or negative, provides a hidden opportunity to grow in self-confidence.

Chapter 11

What do your words say about you?

━ ━ ━ ▬ ▓

Monday 2 January, 10.25 a.m.

'I just don't want to be standing at the funeral in the front row with everybody passing judgement on why I didn't contact my mother when she was dying.'

Steve was thinking aloud, but Lynn was doing all she could to ease his troubled mind.

'They're more likely to talk about you if you stay away,' she replied.

'And I'm not having my Aunt Pat lecture me about what a wonderful man her brother was,' Steve continued. 'He may have been a wonderful brother to her, but he was a lousy father to me.'

'You need to be there, Steve,' suggested Lynn. 'You have to put your differences behind you, otherwise you'll be wracked with guilt for the rest of your life.'

'And I'll tell you what else I don't want to happen,' began Steve, but Lynn interrupted.

'Steve, just concentrate on what you do *want to happen.'*

Steve stopped in his tracks. He looked perplexed by the challenge.

'You know, Lynn, I really don't know what I want,' he finally replied.

Steve's phone lit up with a message:

> what do your words say about you?

'Not helpful,' said Steve. 'I've got enough on my mind without thinking about this nonsense.'

'Well, perhaps it could be helpful, Steve,' suggested Lynn. 'Just think about it for a minute. What do *your words say about you?'*

'Well, right now, my words say nothing about me – because I don't know what I want to do,' he answered.

'But you're allowed to be unsure,' replied Lynn. 'It's impossible to know the answer to everything. In fact, I worry about people who pretend to. So it's OK if you don't know.

'But I would say you have to stop concentrating on what you don't *want. That's the problem. The solution can be found in what you* do *want.'*

'OK,' began Steve. 'I want to have a clear conscience. I want people to understand why we fell out. I don't want any further bad feeling.'

'Well, two out of three's OK,' teased Lynn.

''What do you mean?' asked Steve.

'Firstly, you want a clear conscience and, secondly, you want people to understand. But you don't want bad feeling – so what do you want?'

'I just want to get on with what little family I have left,' Steve rephrased.

'Right,' said Lynn. 'That's three things you *do* want. So how can you achieve that?'

'Well, I'm not phoning Aunt Pat to grovel,' snarled Steve.

'You're being negative again,' corrected Lynn. 'Tell me instead what you will do.'

'OK, I'll phone her and say I'll try to come to the funeral,' started Steve, 'and explain that Mum refused to speak to me for the last two years.'

'Wait a minute, Steve,' replied Lynn. 'Are you going to the funeral … or will you try to go?'

'I'll see,' said Steve half-heartedly.

'Steve, you must make a commitment,' answered Lynn. 'Decide to go … or decide to stay away. But for goodness' sake, don't say you'll "try"!'

'Well, that means I can decide at the last minute,' said Steve.

'That's my point,' fired back Lynn. 'You're refusing to commit – which I have to say you do every time you phone me to say you'll "try" to be home by eight.'

'Well, it's the traffic, Lynn,' Steve started. 'You can never …

But Lynn interrupted. 'No, it's the pub Steve. You never know how long you'll be in the pub.'

Steve was stunned.

'I really don't mind if you stop off for a drink on the way home, but for God's sake be honest with me,' said Lynn. 'My father would always hide behind weasel words like "try" and "do my best" when he was unwilling to commit to me. In the end, I refused to trust a word he said to me – and I'd hate us to reach that stage, Steve.'

'Lynn, I'm sorry,' began Steve. 'I've really struggled the last few months and I haven't really coped very well.'

Steve hesitated, attempting to prevent the tears – but they came anyway.

Lynn put her arms round his neck and hugged him tightly.

'I understand, Steve,' she said. 'Really I do. I just want to help you, rather than be pushed away by you. Let me in to your problems and we'll tackle them together.'

Steve just nodded, still unable to find the words.

That evening, 6.30 p.m.

A brisk walk on a cold, sunny afternoon had put the three of them in good spirits.

Nicky was tired and ready for bed, so Steve looked after his son while Lynn made dinner.

Over a chicken casserole, Lynn returned to the morning's conversation.

'That was an interesting question: What do your words say about you?' she began.

'Well, I was going to make a point,' replied Steve, 'about what your *words say about* you, Lynn.'

'Oh yeah?' she said apprehensively.

'Well, you were on at me to be positive instead of negative about the funeral – but you're negative about yourself,' he began. 'I mean, when I say I like your new jeans, you tell me they were half price in Next.'

'I just like a bargain,' protested Lynn.

'Hang on,' Steve persisted. 'When I say I like your new bracelet, you tell me it was £6.99. And when I say I like your hair, you tell me it needs a cut. What's that all about?'

Lynn was stumped and simply shrugged her shoulders.

'Well, I'll tell you,' said Steve. 'It's about feeling that you're unworthy of the praise.'

Lynn was about to hit back, but instead paused: 'Well, I get embarrassed when people heap praise on me and I feel it's, well, insincere.'

'So when I don't notice your new dress,' asked Steve, 'how do you feel?'

'Disappointed,' she replied. 'Sometimes hurt.'

'And when I do notice?' probed Steve. 'You reject the compliment. You have to accept sincere compliments. Bank them, as you would money. Then, when you're lacking confidence in your appearance, you can draw on what you've banked.'

'So what am I meant to say when you say, "Nice dress"?' asked Lynn.

'You say, "Thank you",' replied Steve.

'Mmm,' acknowledged Lynn. 'So who told you that?'

'Craig told me the day he was appointed as my boss that when he paid me a compliment, he meant it to be accepted,' said Steve. 'I was rather inclined before then to shrug off his praise. So he asked me if he handed me a hundred quid for a job well done, would I throw it back at him? I said that of course I wouldn't. So he then asked why I was so quick to throw back his compliments for a job well done. I couldn't explain it – but Craig could. He said it was because, deep down, I still didn't feel I was "good enough". And I reckon that goes for you, too, Lynn.'

'OK, my turn,' said Lynn. 'Every time I ask how you are, you say, "Not bad".'

'And your point is?' said Steve.

'"Not bad" is more of your negative thinking,' said Lynn.

'So what should I say?' asked Steve.

'You could say, "I'm good, thanks. How are you?"'

'Oh come on. Don't go all "Californian" on me,' said Steve in a phoney mid-Atlantic accent. 'Surely we don't have to pretend we're "fantastic" all the time?'

'Certainly not,' replied Lynn. 'When you're tired, say you're tired. When you're ill, say you're ill. But when you're good, for goodness' sake say you're good!'

'OK then,' volunteered Steve, 'here's another one for you. You can never talk about your attributes without qualifying them.'

'Like what?' asked Lynn.

'Well,' explained Steve, *'you'll say you're "fairly" experienced in your job – or "relatively" confident when presenting – or "quite" good on the computer.'*

'Well, I don't want to appear arrogant,' protested Lynn.

'What's arrogant about saying that you're experienced in your job – confident when presenting – and good on the computer?' asked Steve. *'You're just stating fact. It's as wrong to underplay your ability as it is to overplay it. Just get rid of all these self-deprecating words!'*

'But don't you think people will see me as a big-head?' Lynn asked.

'No, they'll see you as being capable and confident – which is surely what any employer wants.'

The power of words

Everything we say is a reflection of our thoughts, feelings and behaviour.

The specific language we use speaks volumes about how we view ourselves, as well as the world around us.

Words have the power to influence whether we get what we want from a situation and shape our destiny.

They can be used to **wound, criticize and control** or to **encourage, support and inspire** ourselves and those who hear them.

Therefore, we need to choose our words wisely and with great care for they are more powerful tools for change than we could ever imagine.

The tool of talking together

Steve is in conflict over whether to attend his mother's funeral.

Her sudden death has brought to the surface all sorts of unresolved family issues.

He's paralysed by doubt over what to do. As she talks with him, Lynn realizes he's struggling to decide what it is that he wants to achieve out of this difficult family situation.

As they've recently started to do, Lynn and Steve engage in a deeper and more meaningful dialogue about their lives than the superficial conversations of the past few years. This is great progress in their relationship and they're already beginning to reap the benefits as they start to problem-solve together.

At the simplest level, talking things over with people whose views and opinions we trust and value clarifies thinking and feelings. Out of this, a plan of action can take shape.

Talking, as a means of conflict resolution, is a basic and essential life skill.

After talking it through, Steve reaches a conclusion – the first decision in his new action plan.

To make lasting progress, they'll need to make 'talking things through' a *habit*.

Already, this process of improved communication at a deeper level is helping them both to cope better and is building their self-confidence.

The importance of positive self-talk

The words we habitually use impact profoundly on *our communi-cation with ourselves*.

They have the power to affect us positively or negatively. They change the way we feel, make us feel good or bad, lower or raise our mood, discourage or inspire us, build our self-confidence or undermine it.

We must choose our words with great care as they have the ability to empower or to disable us.

This principle holds true in all situations and operates constantly.

But it becomes particularly relevant when we are faced with a problem to solve.

And Steve has one now.

The difficulty is that Steve is currently talking to himself – and to Lynn – about the problem situation confronting them, using nega-tive words and language.

He repeatedly uses negative talk:

> *'I **don't** want to …'*
> *'I'm **not** having …'*
> *'I'm **not** phoning …'*
> *'You can **never** …'*

By talking in this way, Steve is sending his mind unhelpful mes-sages.

Without realizing it, he's downloading inferior software into his mind's computer.

The result is that he's **more** likely to bring about the results he wants to **avoid** and less likely to help him find the **right** solutions.

Empowering words

Steve needs to load the **quality** software of **positive self-talk** into his mind's computer.

Positive programming produces positive results.

Using positive words and language are part of the **quality software** needed to help Steve reach clear decisions about what he wants to achieve. It also helps him bring about the eventual fulfilment of his wishes and contributes towards a successful outcome.

Focusing his mind on what he **wants** to happen and **talking** to himself in language that supports his goals **increases** the chances of success.

It will transform his **thinking**, **feelings** and **behaviour** by turning Steve's:

> **Fear into anticipation;**
> **Negative thoughts into positive thinking;**
> **Disabling behaviour into empowering action.**

Conquering the inner critic

Lynn's inability to take a compliment is a reflection of her negative self-talk and poor self-worth.

When Steve compliments her on her looks or on what she is wearing or on her ability at work, she responds in a self-effacing manner. Compliments just seem to make her feel even more uncomfortable about herself.

Sometimes she convinces herself that he's just complimenting her to be kind.

But why, when Steve is simply telling her the truth?

This is because praise from others **clashes** with her own negative self-talk.

It does not 'fit' with the way in which she speaks to herself inwardly and with the poor image of herself she clings on to, because her inner critic – or green goblin – talks to her in language that constantly puts her down.

When she receives a compliment from the external world, her goblin responds immediately, strongly and harshly sometimes, to rubbish, negate and minimize the praise as quickly as possible.

As a consequence, the compliments have no time to take root and allow self-worth to grow!

Lynn's goblin causes her to underplay her abilities, misrepresent herself, undersell herself, to constantly qualify, minimize and even to dismiss her accomplishments altogether.

In addition, it plays a significant part in her dislike of and ongoing dissatisfaction with her own body. It fuels her misperception of it as being 'unattractive' – something Steve most certainly disagrees with.

Believing and banking

The way forward for Lynn and Steve is to become more aware of the type of language they use when they communicate inwardly with themselves, talk together or when they speak to others.

As Steve rightly suggests, they need to start *believing* and *banking* positive self-talk, genuine compliments and praise.

This can be achieved by them:

> **Becoming more aware** *of their choice and use of negative words*
> **Substituting** *them with positive alternatives*
> **Replacing** *self-deprecating talk with life-affirming self-talk, and*
> **Transforming** *disabling thinking into life-enhancing communication*

Lynn and Steve can start to use **language** that supports the positive life-enhancing beliefs and confident behaviour that they want to create in order to do this.

With Steve and Lynn both due to return to work the next day after their New Year break – and tired from their long afternoon walk – they decided to turn in early.

Steve felt he had resolved some key issues. He would go to his mum's funeral – and he would be happy to tell anybody that it had been her decision to stop speaking to him.

There was, however, one piece of unfinished business.

'Lynn, I'm sorry that I've been less than honest about going to the pub,' he began.

'Steve …' Lynn started.

'No, hear me out,' he continued. 'It started as just a quick pint to relax after a hard day, but it's become a habit as the Bulldog's been snarling at me for months. But I've been thinking about it this evening and I'm going to come straight home from now on and stop making excuses. Quite frankly, if we can talk about these things like we have been the last few weeks, then that'll do me much more good than drowning my sorrows. Hopefully, I'll try to play five-a-side more often instead of just slumping in front of the TV.'

'Hopefully *you'll* try *to play?'* teased Lynn. *'Go on – make a com-mitment!'*

'OK, I will *play five-a-side more often.'* Steve smiled.

'Then it's a plan,' concluded Lynn.

Chapter 12

How are you at solving problems?

— — — ▪▪

Monday 30 January, 7 a.m.

The alarm clock's persistent ring gave Steve little option. He had to get up.

As he pushed the bedroom curtain aside, he could see steady rain piercing the darkness, illuminated by the amber hue of the fluorescent street lighting.

'Oh God,' he mumbled, still half-asleep. 'What a miserable morning.'

He was surprised to find the kitchen light on and Lynn sitting at the breakfast bar, already dressed. She had paperwork scattered in front of her.

'Why are you up so early?' he asked, screwing up his eyes against the harsh light.

'Oh, I'm delivering that new internal communications course today – alone!' Lynn replied. 'I'm just wanting to read through it again before I set off.'

'Are you worried about it?' Steve enquired.

'No, I just want to feel well prepared,' she replied. 'But I'm feeling confident.'

Steve had been reaching for the milk in the fridge, but stopped in his tracks.

'You're feeling what?' he asked.

'Confident,' replied Lynn.

'Not reasonably confident?' probed Steve.

Lynn laughed. 'No, confident – based on good preparation and a healthy level of self-belief!'

'You're going to beat me in the race to become a north-easterner on that compass, aren't you?' suggested Steve.

'Who said it was a race?' replied Lynn. 'I thought it was a journey.'

'Well, you seem a lot happier these days,' observed Steve. 'If it's a journey, I feel I'm dragging my feet – because the prospect of going to work right now holds little attraction, especially on a wet Monday morning in January.'

'I do feel better,' said Lynn. 'It feels as if the changes I've made are reaping benefits.'

'Wish I could say the same,' said Steve.

That morning, 7.45 a.m.

As he drove through the gloom – both of the winter's morning and of his state of mind – a light brightened the inside of the car. It was his mobile phone with a message:

How are you at solving problems?

Steve placed the phone back down and sighed wearily.

'Apparently not very good,' he answered.

His thoughts turned to which particular problems he had had to solve recently.

Top of his list was his over-indulgence in drink. But, in fairness, he had made a commitment to Lynn four weeks ago and had stuck to his side of the bargain. Only once had he gone to the pub on the way home – but that was for a colleague's farewell drink.

Then there was the issue of his mother's funeral. He had gone to the funeral and received a surprisingly warm reception from relatives who had last seen him some years before.

In fact, they'd shared Steve's views on his father – but admitted openly that they had lacked the courage to voice their opinions. A cousin had also said that she had found Steve's mum very abrasive in her latter years and blamed her for causing friction throughout the family.

Steve had enjoyed seeing some of his family so much that he'd asked several of them to dinner next month.

Then there was his work. Well, what a contrast between the spring in Lynn's step and the ball and chain round his ankles.

The more he thought about it, however, the more he remembered how uncertain Lynn had been about returning to work and the pressures of being a working mum. Yet she had got through these doubts and now felt confident – for the first time in her working life.

'If I could only sort out the Bulldog,' Steve considered, *'my life would be so different.'*

That evening, 6.30 p.m.

'Hi, Gorgeous!' greeted Steve, as he gave Lynn a lingering hug. *'How's my boy?'* he asked, lifting up Nicky to embrace them both together, warmly.

'You seem unusually bright,' observed Lynn. *'At least, compared to your mood this morning.'*

'Well, I got a text today,' said Steve. *'How are you at solving problems?'*

'I'd say you're good,' offered Lynn.

'And I'd agree,' replied Steve. *'But I've been dodging the biggest problem in my life and today I decided I'm going to resolve it one way or the other.'*

'You're leaving me for another woman?' joked Lynn.

'Beggars can't be choosers,' fired back Steve.

'So what are you going to do?' asked Lynn. *'Poison the Bulldog's blueberry muffin?'*

'No, I'm going to speak to him about it,' replied Steve. *'But, first, I'm going to call my team together – apologize for being overbearing – and motivate them to roll up their sleeves and pull together. Second, I'm going to work my butt off this next month to get some sales in. Finally, I'm going to ask for a meeting with Dave, demonstrate the improvement and tell him to cut me some slack.'*

'Wow!' said Lynn. *'Have you been swallowing the bravery pills?'*

'No,' replied Steve, *'I've just worked out how to deal with my biggest problem.'*

'And what if he tells you to bugger off?' asked Lynn.

'I'll cross that bridge when I come to it.'

'Well, you certainly look a lot happier tonight,' Lynn suggested.

'I feel better,' he replied. *'But anyway, how did your course go?'*

'Really well,' said Lynn. *'I felt good when I stood up and I reckon the group fed off how I was feeling.'*

'So, no panic attacks, no hot flushes, no stuttering with nerves?' Steve asked.

'No, I'd even go as far as to say that I enjoyed it,' concluded Lynn.

Recognizing the problem

Problems are part of life and Lynn and Steve, just like every one of us, have their fair share.

Everyone has problems to deal with, but successful and confident people handle them better. Learning to solve problems has the potential to build confidence and coping skills.

Problems in themselves are neither 'good' nor 'bad'. It's how we deal with them that really matters.

How we RESPOND to the problems is what REALLY matters.

For some time now, they've both been struggling along, doing the best that they can and it's only recently that they've begun to open up and to communicate together in a meaningful way about the difficulties they've been hiding from one another.

In other words, their *self-awareness* is increasing.

More important still, they are each coming to realize the individual problems that they've been *keeping secret even from themselves*.

Admittedly, at the beginning, opening up to one another was a very scary experience, particularly for Steve. This increased self-awareness caused him to recognize specific problems for the first time in his life.

Initially, it felt as if he was developing *new* problems – that things were getting worse rather than better.

However, once he understood the difficulties and saw the big picture more clearly, things rapidly improved.

Increasing self-awareness initially makes us feel uncomfortable, but it is the gateway to change and personal growth.

It was Lynn who pointed out that his problems with his father, his family, his driven-ness, his drinking, with Dave the Bulldog, and even in his relationship with Lynn herself, had been there all along. He had just not stopped long enough to notice.

In relation to some problems, though, Steve had been in *denial*.

Other problems he simply chose to *ignore*, hoping they might disappear.

But *denial* and *ignoring* are methods of coping that rarely work for long. They certainly fail in solving problems, building confidence and finding personal happiness. In the long term, they are disempowering rather than enabling.

In a sense, Steve has been protecting himself by refusing to accept some of the difficulties, or to appreciate their full extent and the detrimental effect they are having on his family and colleagues.

As long as he stayed in that state of 'blindness', however, there was little to no chance of him solving any problems whatsoever.

Before we can begin to solve a problem, we first have to recognize and accept its existence.

Although glaringly obvious, this is often surprisingly difficult to do.

All along, the clues to the fact they had problems were there, if Lynn and Steve were only willing to pause long enough and look with open minds.

Sometimes, though, it takes a personal crisis to occur to stop us in our tracks and to cause us to question our lives deeply enough.

Sometimes we need to stop and take stock, to examine our behaviour and our deepest feelings in order to discover where we are and what's happening in our lives.

Understanding the problem

Understanding problems can be a challenge, particularly when they first present themselves.

Lynn and Steve had each started to think about their problems when on their own. However, there's a limit to the usefulness of this personal reflection as a way of solving problems. Sometimes things just go round and round inside our heads and do not take us any further forward.

The best progress Steve and Lynn have made so far in problem solving has come when they started to talk together.

Although, at first, opening up to one another felt 'risky', it has been an exciting breakthrough in their relationship and they sense it as they laugh and joke together more than they have in a long time.

And it's clearly getting easier for them to practise, especially now that they are beginning to appreciate the benefits.

Lynn is definitely feeling happier and more confident, particularly at work. And Steve is feeling more hopeful about the future as he begins to see a possible way forward.

One secret to understanding a problem is to ask ourselves the right questions.

Steve and Lynn are learning this skill from the mysterious text messages they are receiving in the form of searching questions. They're beginning to appreciate that asking the right questions is the way to start solving their problems.

The best questions produce the best kind of answers.

One of the difficulties has been that, for some time now, Lynn has been asking herself poor-quality questions, such as:

What's wrong with me?
Why can't I lose weight?
Who's to blame?

Similarly, Steve has been asking himself unhelpful questions:

What's the point in trying any more?
Why me?
How could he do this to me?

Lynn and Steve need to focus their minds on asking meaningful questions that will lead them forward towards possible meaningful solutions.

And they are starting to do it now.

Questions such as:

> **What exactly is the problem here?**
> **Where is the 'up' side to this problem?**
> **What is the 'down' side to this problem?**
> **What do I want from this situation?**
> **How could I make this situation work for me?**
> **How can I turn things around for the better?**
> **What – and who – matters most to me in my life right now?**
> **What am I ready to do right now to improve things?**
> **What am I prepared to consider doing in the future to improve things?**
> **What should I refuse to put up with any more?**
> **What do I have to change about my thinking and behaviour to empower me?**

Asking the right questions will help Steve and Lynn to understand the true nature of their difficulties, and enable them to start formulating a plan for dealing with them.

Meaningful questions bring the problem into sharper focus.

Developing an action plan

Recognizing their problems and *understanding* the nature of them are moving Steve and Lynn forwards towards solving them.

Steve has already given his work problem with Dave some thought and has devised a plan.

He's been asking himself some searching questions and is clearer in his mind about the situation:

> **What does he want?** *– To get Dave off his back.*

What should he refuse to put up with any longer? – *Dave's persistent bullying, which is eroding his self-worth and confidence.*

What he is prepared to do next? – *He has put together a provisional action plan.*

— — — — ▪

Later that evening

'You know, it's almost the reverse for me,' began Lynn, as Steve watched the highlights of another inglorious United failure in the league.

Steve hit the Live Pause button on his Sky Plus and turned to Lynn, giving her his full attention.

'Sorry, what were you saying?'

'My situation's the reverse of yours, as far as problem-solving is concerned,' began Lynn again, 'because I'm much happier at work, but I'm still struggling with guilt.'

'Guilt about what?' asked Steve.

'Guilt about being firmer with mum, guilt about having less time with Nicky, guilt about pruning back my friends,' Lynn expanded.

'Well, your mum is getting her shopping online and you now pop in at weekends,' said Steve. 'And she's seeing more of Nicky when you leave him there while you're at yoga. Nicky's seeing more of his doting gran – and really enjoying school. And your pals are now aware that friendship involves listening as well as talking, which, for them, is a newly acquired skill!'

'I suppose it sounds reasonable when you put it that way,' reflected Lynn.

'Lynn, you had to find time for yourself – and look how you're enjoying yoga,' continued Steve. 'And, if you don't mind me saying, you're looking rather tasty and well toned these days.'

'As opposed to what?' asked Lynn in fake indignation.

'As opposed to being rather tasty … but less well toned,' replied Steve, thinking quickly.

'Right,' said Lynn, 'seeing as my muscle groups meet your approval, how about improving your mental muscle?'

'What do you suggest?' asked Steve.

'Let's get your brain in shape for a meeting with Dave by rehearsing your chat with him,' she continued. 'You tell me how he'll behave and I'll play his part in a role play.'

'Mmm,' said Steve sceptically.

'We do role plays all the time at work,' insisted Lynn. 'You'll really benefit from thinking this conversation through.'

'OK,' said Steve. 'But you'll have to put on 10 stone to look the part.'

'Enough nonsense,' said Lynn. 'Sit down and write down all the points he'll try to score against you. Start with Regret, Reason and Remedy.'

'What's that?' asked Steve, perplexed.

'Well, you want to take the moral high ground in the conversation with Dave to ensure he doesn't start picking off your weak arguments. So start by saying you're sorry he's been disappointed in your performance – go through the reasons as to why it's been difficult – and tell him how you'll sort it out. It's a technique called Regret, Reason and Remedy.'

'He'll just pounce on an apology as a sign of weakness,' said Steve.

'It's a sign of strength,' replied Lynn. 'It's weak people who can never bring themselves to apologize. We all have failings. Only strong people recognize them.'

'Regret, reason, remedy,' reiterated Steve. 'I'll remember that.'

'Of course, you'll have to practise getting that word "sorry" across your lips in the first place,' she added.

'Cheeky!' concluded Steve.

_ _ _ _ _

Brainstorming

Lynn's right to put some brakes on Steve's enthusiasm.

She senses Steve could rush ahead too hastily, before he has sufficiently thought through all the different solutions and their possible consequences.

She recognizes that they need to do some brainstorming together on the possible solutions and draw up a more detailed final plan before putting it into action.

Her role-playing idea is one excellent way of achieving both these aims simultaneously.

The problems are not yet solved and the plan may not yet be perfected but it's certainly taking shape. This brings a feeling of relief and some immediate benefits.

Both Lynn and Steve are feeling a lot happier, less confused and more in control of their lives.

Chapter 13

Are you acting 'as if'?

━ ━ ━ ━ ■

Tuesday 14 February, 11.40 a.m.

For someone whose 'door is always open', the Bulldog's door had remained tightly shut to Steve in the fortnight since he'd asked for a chat.

The timing was ironic, Steve reckoned. He had a Valentine's date with a man in love – with himself.

As he walked towards Dave's office, Steve pulled back his shoulders, stiffened his back and began smiling. Dave's secretary smiled back, without realizing that Steve was only warming up on her.

Before entering the office, Steve ran through his bullet points one more time in his head.

'Regret, reason, remedy … refuse to rise to the bait … maintain eye contact … answer questions directly … keep my cool … come out smiling,' he rehearsed to himself.

His mind went back to the two evenings with Lynn in which she had fired all Dave's barbs at him and he had resisted the pres-

sure. He now had some protection against the hail of bullets he expected to face.

He'd done the preparation. Now he just had to perform.

'Come in!' barked the Bulldog, a second after Steve knocked.

Dave remained seated behind his screen, feverishly knocking out an email on the keyboard, as Steve stood in front of the desk. After a few seconds of silence, Steve decided to sit.

'This will take a couple of minutes,' said Dave, still battering away. With a triumphant flourish, he hit the send button.

'That'll give him something to think about,' threatened Dave.

For just a second, Steve considered the possibility that it was all an act and there was no lucky recipient.

'Now, you wanted to see me,' said Dave, leaning back in his leather seat, placing both his hands behind his head and stretching his elbows out.

'Yes indeed,' began Steve confidently, 'and thanks for making the time. As you know, Dave, I've been disappointed with my figures for the past few months …'

'And you're not the only one …' interrupted Dave, preparing for a monologue. But Steve pressed on:

'And I acknowledge that's put a strain on you and on my own team, which is why I apologized to them last week – and now I want you to know I'm sorry I've been underperforming.'

Dave hesitated and thought of offering words of consolation, but instead opted for a snarl.

'Well, there's no point apologizing after the event,' he began. 'It's too late by then.'

'On the contrary,' began Steve. 'It's the only time. But I simply wanted to explain what had happened and let you know what I've done about it.'

The Bulldog sat impassively, waiting for the first flaw in the argument.

Steve continued. 'For whatever reason, I feel I've lost ground these last few months. I've worked as hard, but the results have dried up. A bit like United really,' he joked, weakly.

Dave drew breath, but Steve got in first.

'Anyway, I've had a better fortnight – which will show in next month's figures – and you can rest assured the improvement will be constant.'

So far, so good. The Bulldog seemed pacified, but Steve was still on his guard.

'So you can guarantee improved figures?' was Dave's calculating response.

'No,' Steve began.

'No!' interrupted Dave.

'No, what I can guarantee,' continued Steve, 'is a commitment to the job and to my team. I'm convinced the promising results of the last two weeks will continue.'

'So, no guarantee?' toyed Dave.

'My guarantee is one of commitment,' hit back Steve, 'and that way I believe we'll get the results.'

The Bulldog tried another line of attack.

'And what if the results don't come?' he asked, barely able to suppress a cruel smile.

'I believe they will come,' returned Steve.

'But if they don't,' pressed Dave, 'what then? Can I expect your resignation on my desk?'

Steve hesitated.

'Well?' barked the Bulldog.

Steve resisted the temptation to fold like the child so bullied by his father.

'Absolutely not,' replied Steve. 'That's too easy an option. I want to fight to see the job done and turn things around. That is what I believe I can do.'

'Well, for your sake, I hope you're right,' concluded Dave.

'For everybody's sake, I want to get it right,' concluded Steve. 'And thanks again for your time, Dave.'

Steve reached out his right hand, offering Dave little alternative but to accept the handshake. The Bulldog even found himself offering a weak smile in reply to the broad one afforded him by Steve.

The former Regional Sales Director of the Year bounced to the car park, greeting each employee he encountered on the way.

Safely inside the Mondeo, he pressed No. 1 on his mobile's speed dial list and waited for Lynn to answer.

After two rings, she duly did, recognizing Steve's number.

'Well?' she asked in anticipation.

'He's an ignorant …' Steve began.

'Well we know that, but how did it go?' she insisted.

'Surprisingly well,' began Steve. 'He tried the "guarantee" question we rehearsed and he pulled the old "will you resign?" stunt – but the rehearsal paid off because I took the moral high ground each time.'

'Brilliant!' shrieked Lynn. 'But do you still have a job?'

'Absolutely,' replied Steve. 'And it's the first time I've stood up to Dave and left the meeting feeling better than when I went in.'

'That's terrific!' said Lynn. 'I'll hear more about it tonight, before our candlelit dinner. What time will you be home?'

'By seven,' came the certain reply. 'See you then – and thanks, Lynn.'

'For what?' she asked.

'For believing in me when I didn't,' came the surprisingly frank reply.

'My pleasure,' said Lynn. 'See you tonight, handsome.'

As Lynn hung up, her mobile indicated a new message:

Are you acting as if …?

'As if what?' asked Lynn out loud.

Preparation

Steve is determined to succeed in overcoming his problem with the Bulldog.

And he's going about it the right way.

At one time, it would have been so easy for him to have let this situation bring him down even further than it already has, causing him to 'burn out'.

He could have done nothing, let the pattern of destructive bullying continue and found himself ill or driven out of his job.

Even now, he could choose to let his fears overpower and paralyse him. There are still mornings when he's afraid to get out of bed and days when he has to work up the courage to make the lonely pilgrimage from his car to the office door.

But Steve's beginning to change. His courage is becoming bigger than his fear. Steve is developing *self-belief*.

Thinking about the text messages, in combination with his discussions with Lynn, has increased his self-awareness. This increased understanding of himself has made him more aware of the heart of the problem he has with Dave.

In turn, this has enabled him to draw up a more effective problem-solving plan in order to deal with it.

Steve has been empowered to take appropriate action.

When it comes to success in any new venture, a reasonable degree of self-belief is essential because what we believe about ourselves and our abilities affects the possible outcome in any given situation. In this sense, we create our own destiny.

Our power to solve problems is limited only by the strength of our belief that we can.

If we believe that we *can*, then we're more likely to succeed. If we believe that we *can't*, then we'll also probably be right too.

The power of the mind is that it tends towards creating what it believes.

But self-belief has to be soundly based on *preparation*, *performance* and *physiology*, otherwise it is merely a false sense of security.

Facing a challenge unprepared would be like walking into the gladiatorial arena without having mastered the skills of hand-to-hand combat; or going to sit an examination without having studied adequately; or attending an interview without having done our homework and honed our interview technique.

And yet we've all done this at one time or another and then been surprised when things don't work out!

Steve's preparation has suddenly made him aware, for the first time, of the personal buttons Dave's been pressing – the legacy of his relationship with his critical bullying father and his eternal striving to please him.

Steve has been behaving towards Dave AS IF he were his father.

This is the '*hook*' that Dave has had in Steve and explains why he was brought to the edge of despair. Dave's bullying has been such a powerful and destructive weapon because it's touched this painful raw nerve in Steve.

Performance

Equally important for Steve was the need to *perform* well on the day of his meeting with Dave.

And in order to build his belief that he could handle it, Steve needed to *practise* how he would play it.

This is why Lynn's suggestion of role playing his forthcoming showdown with Dave was so helpful. The idea scared Steve witless at first but the experience proved worth its weight in gold on this, his first day of reckoning with Dave.

Practice enables us to connect up what we KNOW we have to do with the actual DOING of it.

This is because practice creates the unique *mind–body connections* essential for executing successfully the specific behaviour we want to develop.

For example, even though a musician has memorized the melodies, notes and musical arrangements of a piece, he would only go on stage to perform having practised them over and over again on the instrument – in private or, better still, on a stage without the audience present.

These vital mind–body connections are the equivalent of powerful *confidence motorways* along which we can travel easily, effortlessly, confidently and with self-belief.

This is true of any behaviour pattern we may wish to develop or reinforce, such as behaving more confidently, playing a musical instrument, speaking in public or, in Steve's situation, the performance strategy for his forthcoming encounter with Dave.

In this way, the whole 'performance' becomes confident, natural, effortless and, ultimately, much more powerful.

Role playing with Lynn allowed Steve the opportunity to 'hear and see' his own performance in advance. In addition, it provided the benefit of external input and opinion from Lynn, who has the advantage of being objective and only having Steve's best interests at heart.

If Lynn had not come up with the idea of role playing, then practising in front of a mirror or using a camera to record the 'rehearsal' would have been effective alternatives that Steve could have used.

Physiology

Preparation and practice are important in creating confident behaviour, but developing a healthy *physiology* is also vital.

And both Steve and Lynn are beginning to improve their *physiology* by enhancing their physical health and fitness.

Lynn has started yoga classes and Steve is back playing five-a-side football and going to the gym. In addition to being fitter, they are eating more healthily and drinking less alcohol. She feels calmer and less stressed and his mood has lifted.

Their general sense of physical and emotional well-being has been given a huge boost and they both wish that they had started being more active much sooner.

For Steve, bringing a healthier body to the preparation, practice and performance situations has powerfully enhanced the learning process itself and ultimately the quality of the confident behaviour and self-belief he has created.

This is because it helps to build the large and robust confidence motorways between mind and body, necessary for the confident behaviour to become '*hard wired*'.

Working with an unfit body and eating unhealthily is akin to entering a standard saloon car in the Monaco Grand Prix, filling it with low-grade fuel and then expecting it to perform well and have a real chance of winning.

The confidence spiral

But Steve is also beginning to use his body language to enhance his confidence and self-belief in another effective way – by **acting as if** he feels confident.

This involves him using good body language to create a state of confidence and self-belief by changing things like his facial expression, breathing, posture, stance and movement to those associated with confident behaviour.

He walks into the meeting with Dave with his shoulders back and smiles as he confidently and firmly shakes his hand. He speaks clearly and loudly enough, while keeping good eye contact.

This behaviour sends powerful '**confident messages**' to his brain through the confidence motorways he's been building during role play.

The more he acts as if he is confident, the more confidence he will genuinely begin to experience.

Steve is experiencing the powerful connections between:

> *body and mind*
> *physiology and feelings*
> *behaving confidently and feeling confident*
> *acting as if he's confident and experiencing a state of confidence*

This is the power of the mind–body connection – to create *confidence motorways* between the way we behave and the way we think and feel.

Acting as if we are confident puts us in a more confident state. When we feel more confident we behave in a more confident manner and, as we repeat this cycle, we send our confidence on an upward spiral.

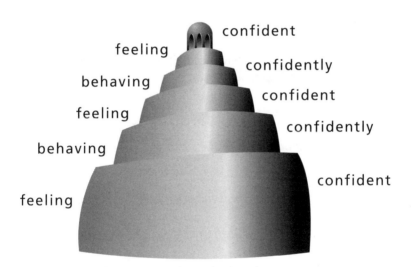

That evening

As good as his word, Steve was in the flat at 6.45, carrying a large bouquet of flowers.

'These are magnificent,' gasped Lynn.

'If only they were for you,' Steve teased, putting them behind his back. *'Happy Valentine's Day!'*

With Nicky at his gran's house for the night, there was nobody to interrupt their lengthy embrace.

'I just wish I didn't have that interview tomorrow to put me off my food tonight,' said Lynn.

'We'll rehearse it over dinner,' suggested Steve.

'How romantic!' replied Lynn.

'Well, you have to be positive,' said Steve. *'You have to act as if the job's got your name written on it.'*

'Act as if …?' asked Lynn.

'Sure, if you're uncertain, just act as if you were confident,' replied Steve.

'I got a text with these words this afternoon,' said Lynn.

'Ah, the Phantom of the Soap Opera,' suggested Steve.

Twenty minutes later, Lynn was in her black dress and standing in front of the full-length mirror in the bedroom.

'I can just see a horrible bump where my tummy used to be,' she groaned, holding her hand on her stomach.

Steve stood behind her and put his arms round her, looking at them both in the mirror.

His paunch had reduced and the double chin was back to a single. His regular five-a-side football nights were also now supplement-ed by a once-a-week trip to the gym.

'I can just see an incredibly attractive woman with a great personality, a bundle load of compassion who's a terrific wife and mother – whom I love to bits,' he said, squeezing her tight.

They were the kind of words that, until recently, she had expected never to hear from him again.

━ ━ ━ ━ ▓

Chapter 14

Does your mind work for you?

Wednesday 15 February, 2.45 p.m.

Lynn sat in her car, parked outside the bank headquarters, fighting conflicting emotions.

She had presented so well when asked to 'go solo' recently, in front of 50 senior bank delegates. The Finance Director and Corporate Banking boss had both spoken to her afterwards to congratulate her on the excellent delivery.

So why did she always feel her stomach churning before her personal assessment, or any job interview, for that matter? Was it that she hid behind the mask of her job – until the spotlight was on her as a person?

It was as if there were two Lynns. The woman who stood confidently in front of a crowd, presenting on communication – and the little girl who stood cowering in front of the head teacher, waiting for a row.

Her mind drifted off to her childhood, looking for answers.

Her mum tried so hard to boost her confidence. She had always praised her – regardless of how Lynn had done.

Perhaps that was the problem. Perhaps she had stopped believing her mum because there was never a moment when an improvement was suggested. Only praise.

Of course her dad never made it to the school performances or her dancing shows. He seemed to be vaguely interested in her progress, as if he were hearing reports about a distant relative.

So with nothing to judge her mother's lavish praise against, it had become much easier to be sceptical about all compliments. She felt that way she could guard against being 'taken in'.

Lynn had become so much better, though, at accepting compliments about her business presentations. It was the personal ones that still seemed difficult to believe.

And with her inability to 'bank' those, she still felt very exposed when the conversation was about her, rather than the business.

As she locked up the car, Lynn went to remove the flyer on her windscreen.

'Does your mind work for you?' it asked, suggesting that hypnotherapy with Dr Dave DeSilva would help you overcome 'drinking, smoking and fear of flying'.

'Doctor of what?' asked Lynn to nobody in particular.

'I'm so bad in interviews,' she told herself, entering the lift to the sixth floor – boardroom level.

'No, Lynn – stop thinking negatively,' she warned herself. 'You are good at these interviews.'

But the words were hollow. Lynn felt quite squeamish and wished she was anywhere else, other than facing an interview for a promoted post – Head of Training.

As the lift rose, a noise came from her handbag.

'Damn! I meant to switch that off,' she thought, reaching for her phone.

Before silencing it, Lynn read the message:

> Does your mind work for you?

'Yes, but only with the help of a hypnotherapist, apparently,' she said mockingly, causing the young temp sharing the lift with her to look at Lynn strangely.

When Lynn arrived outside the boardroom, one of her interviewers was waiting for her.

Jane Browning, retiring Head of Training, touched Lynn on the arm in a friendly manner.

'Now, I know you get nervous at these wretched interviews,' she said. 'If you want to use a trick I learned a long time ago, think of us all sitting in our pyjamas sporting big Mickey Mouse ears. If you still felt nervous facing a panel like that, I'd eat my hat.'

'Thanks, Jane,' Lynn laughed. 'I'll bear that in mind.'

'Go for it, Lynn. This is your big chance. Show them what I already know,' she said, departing into the boardroom.

It was 10 minutes later, once the other four panel members had arrived, that Lynn was invited in.

She nodded to Jane and the other two she knew – and introduced herself with a handshake to the two unknown to her.

'Lynn, perhaps you can remind us all of what brings you here,' opened the woman Lynn was looking to succeed.

'Well, I was delighted to be asked to apply for this job – and at first I was a little surprised,' Lynn began, teetering on the edge of talking herself out of the post.

'However, having considered what I've been doing since returning full-time last September, I now believe I'm ready for the challenge.'

'Yes, it is only less than six months since you went full-time,' solemnly pointed out the panellist who, peering over his bi-focals, resembled a High Court judge.

'I wonder if you're certain that you wish to remain full-time, or whether you'll want to return to part-time working.'

Lynn caught Jane's eye before answering and noticed her sweeping her hair behind her ears with both hands. She then cupped her hands, to remind Lynn of the Mickey Mouse ears.

Lynn laughed, a little too obviously for her own liking.

'Yes, I have to laugh when I remember dithering about returning,' she began, *' but now, weighing up on a Monday morning whether I wish to breathe life into the presentations of my colleagues or debate with a five-year-old the pros – but mostly cons – of "colouring in" my white bedroom carpet, the former wins hands down each time.'*

The 'judge' smiled. The other four laughed.

'Good start, Lynn,' she told herself. *'Now just stay relaxed and concentrate on the positives.'*

Mind power

Our mind is the most powerful tool we have at our disposal to understand the world about us and to deal with life. It's therefore vital that we make our mind our loyal ally.

In every moment, our own mind is either working for or against us. The choice is ours.

Lynn thinks back to her childhood and how she struggled even then to make sense of her family, her environment and her 'world'.

She now realizes that, in so many ways, it didn't add up at all.

Her mother praised her, irrespective of what she did – and her father gave her no feedback whatsoever, neither good nor bad.

She recognizes how impossible it was, as a child growing up in that specific setting, to construct a clear picture of a rational world.

Suddenly it dawns on her:

> *It's impossible to build a sure sense of healthy self-worth on the shifting sands of inconsistent and conflicting parental messages.*

No wonder Lynn has doubted herself so much and found compliments from Steve and her colleagues hard to believe. She still thinks, sometimes, that they are 'just being nice' to her by not telling her the truth.

Revisiting, re-evaluating and reconstructing

Lynn is realizing how important it is for her now, *as an adult*, to **REVISIT** the erroneous conclusions she came to about herself, *as a child*.

Because, unwittingly, she's been living her *adult life* based on the opinion of herself that she formed *as a child*. And that is outdated and inaccurate.

Lynn fashioned a misshapen view of herself and formed poor beliefs regarding her abilities, as a consequence of growing up in her unique family environment – a result of living on '*Planet Peterson*'!

Her evaluation of herself was strongly influenced by the relationships she had with her parents.

The exciting thing is that, after revisiting her childhood opinions of herself, she is then in a powerful position to *RE-EVALUATE* them in the light of evidence regarding herself that is now available to her.

Our family may have passed a sentence on us as a child, but we can overturn that sentence in our own 'Appeal Court' – based on the new evidence that has since come to light.

The evidence – that she is of greater worth and value than she previously thought – is all around her, if only she looks with a more open mind and is prepared to take on board what she sees.

She can source the evidence and information she needs by asking Steve, friends and work colleagues who clearly hold her in high regard and appreciate her abilities and personal qualities – as a woman, as a mother and as a professional.

By *REVISITING* her beliefs about herself and *RE-EVALUATING* them, Lynn can begin to modify her poor view of herself and *RE-CONSTRUCT* a set of healthier, more accurate and empowering self-beliefs.

In this way, Lynn's self-confidence can grow.

Positive self-talk

Replacing negative self-talk, in the form of unhelpful, disempowering thoughts, with positive self-affirming ones, is an essential life skill that builds self-confidence and increases our chances of success.

Lynn's inner critic, her *'goblin'* as she calls it, always goes into overdrive whenever she's under stress.

And she's been worrying and obsessing over her approaching job interview for days.

For the first time she can remember, Lynn courageously challenges her 'goblin' when it begins its familiar critical monologue and starts to 'run her down'.

When the 'goblin' jibes that she is *'so bad at interviews'*, Lynn helpfully replaces this negative false belief about herself with a more *positive alternative:* *'You are good at these interviews'*.

Although Lynn may feel this is a bit strange and artificial at first, the practice of substituting negative thoughts with empowering alternatives is one she will need to cultivate.

This whole process requires it to become a *habit* before it feels effortless and natural.

As she becomes more aware of her unhelpful thinking style, Lynn makes the choice to start initiating positive self-talk.

At the right time, and when it matters most, she's able to give herself some accurate positive feedback and encouragement during the interview itself:

'Good start, Lynn,' she tells herself, *'now just stay relaxed and concentrate on the positives.'*

By doing this, Lynn is immediately starting to *make her mind work for her* rather than *against her* – and it pays off instantly.

Learning to make our mind our BEST FRIEND and LOYAL SUP-PORTER is essential if we want to discover peace of mind.

Your Mind Map

As we go through each day, we're constantly forming opinions and views of what's happening to us and around us.

And these views form the basis for what we call *'reality'*.

We believe that the information we collect from our senses is truly objective. But really our mind is *squeezing* all the information it is receiving from around us, through the *filter* of our personal beliefs about ourselves and others, based on our past experiences.

This somewhat distorted perception then becomes a picture or version of reality that is unique to each one of us.

In this way, moment by moment, we form our own personal *representation* of our experience.

This is our personal *Mind Map of the World*.

It's our *Mind Map* that we follow as we make our way through each day – when we experience a conversation, an encounter, a meeting, look in the mirror, read the newspaper or go on a journey.

The difficulty is that our Mind Map version of reality may not be 'geographically' accurate, because it's only our personal representation and reconstruction of what we experience.

The Mind Map of the world that Steve forms and follows when he's in the presence of bullying Dave has been blurred by his childhood experiences at the hands of his critical father.

As a result, he did find himself *acting as if* Dave was his father, in a way that was unhelpful to him.

Steve has now formed a much more accurate Mind Map of the situation to follow, since he has become aware of this distortion.

Reframing

One effective way to make our mind work *for us* in difficult situations, rather than *against us*, is to *reframe* our view of events so that they empower us.

Lynn uses this device well during her job interview when she imagines the panel wearing Mickey Mouse ears.

However, using her inaccurate Mind Map of the interview setting, she also views one panel member in a distorted way.

She sees him in her mind as 'the judge' and therefore, by implication, out to sentence her – rather than assess her fairly and appreciate her job qualities.

This is an unhelpful Mind Map to follow in an interview setting but she uses a type of reframing, *visual reframing*, to get her past this obstacle.

She *visually reframes* her picture of the panel in a way that robs 'the judge' of the power she's already granted to him in her mind, by viewing him in a ridiculous way, with huge protruding ears. And it works a treat.

Visually reframing *jolts* her mind out of imagining an unhelpful picture of the situation into working with an empowering one.

Lynn is grasping the enormous personal power at her disposal the moment she starts to **make her mind work for her**.

That afternoon, 4.10 p.m.

'Well, how did it go?' asked Steve tentatively, as Lynn picked up her office phone.

'Actually, very well,' answered Lynn, more positively than Steve had expected.

'Great,' he said. 'So what made the difference this time?'

Lynn took Steve through the conversation with Jane Browning, her reminder of the Mickey Mouse ears, her confident start – and the string of good answers she gave to searching questions.

'Not a "quite" or "fairly" or "hopefully" in sight,' she concluded triumphantly.

'So do you reckon you'll get the job?' asked Steve.

'Well, I have a great chance,' replied Lynn.

'I'm having an interesting day,' said Steve.

'Why, what's happened?' said Lynn.

'Tell you when I get home,' teased Steve – and hung up.

Tuesday, 7.30 p.m.

'This had better be good,' said Lynn, as her husband walked into the kitchen of their flat.

'Well it is, as a matter of fact,' said Steve. 'Do you remember that advert that began "Are you good enough to lead our sales team?"'

'Sure, but that was months ago,' said Lynn.

'Well, the original ad was back in September,' said Steve. 'I came across it in the pocket of my old suit trousers last week and, for some reason, decided to phone them. It turns out the appointment fell through because of a legal wrangle over compensation – and so they're needing a sales director in a hurry.'

'They told you all this on the phone?' asked Lynn, bemused.

'No, the Chief Executive told me when I dropped in at five this evening for a chat,' said Steve, as Lynn's eyes widened. 'He turns out to be an old university friend of mine – Chris Williamson. Lynn, he's offered me the job, based on what I achieved last year. He told me he had thought of calling me when he read about the award.'

Lynn was speechless. So many questions flooded though her head, but only one came out her mouth.

'How much does it pay?'

'Five grand less than I'm on,' said Steve. 'But that would improve, based on performance.'

'Risky,' said Lynn.

'The only risk would be to ignore your gut instinct,' said Steve.

'You're right,' said Lynn. 'So do you want to take it?'

'I've said I'll give him an answer by five tomorrow,' said Steve. 'But first, I'm going to resolve some unfinished business with Dave.'

Thursday 16 February, 8.30 a.m.

'Morning, Dave. Can I have a word?' asked Steve.

'A brief one,' replied Dave, chewing on his breakfast blueberry muffin.

Steve drew up a seat.

'There was something I omitted to say yesterday,' began Steve.

'Oh yeah,' replied Dave, barely interested.

'I've given my commitment to the job – but I require your commitment also,' Steve started.

'My commitment to what?' barked the Bulldog.

'To stop bullying me and everybody else in this company,' continued Steve.

'Are you suggesting I'm a bully?' snarled Dave, the crumbs of blueberry muffin now flying in all directions.

'I'm not suggesting it, Dave. I'm saying directly and unambiguously that you are a bully.'

For once, Dave was confounded, so Steve continued.

'Now, do I have your guarantee that the bullying will stop immediately?' asked Steve.

Dave was about to explode.

'Well, do I?' asked Steve.

'Get out my office right away!' shouted Dave.

'With respect, that's not an answer, Dave. Is the bullying going to stop?'

'Get out!' screamed Dave. 'And consider what you're going to say when I have you disciplined for gross misconduct.'

'I've only asked you politely to stop bullying your staff,' replied Steve. 'It's your misconduct that's gross. So I'll ask a final time, can you guarantee that the bullying will stop or do I have to report your behaviour to the Chief Executive?'

'You wouldn't dare,' snapped Dave.

'Watch me!' replied Steve.

'You'll leave this company before I do,' hit back Dave.

'Well, you're probably right there,' said Steve, pulling a white envelope out of his jacket inside pocket, 'because this is my resignation letter. But I will make it my business to write a formal complaint about your behaviour before I leave. Craig, being the fair man he is, will undoubtedly take that very seriously indeed. Good morning, Dave,' concluded Steve, smiling as he closed the door quietly behind him on the way out.

Twenty minutes later

'No way!' exclaimed Lynn, on hearing Steve's report of the meeting.

She pressed her mobile close to her ear, to make sure she caught every word.

'And you didn't feel nervous?' she asked.

'I envisaged him in his boxer shorts with huge ears – which he has anyway,' replied Steve.

'And what if the new job falls through?' said Lynn, suddenly realizing the consequences of Steve's actions.

'Even if it did – and I'm convinced it'll be confirmed this week – even if it did, I'm still a good candidate for any similar job going,' said Steve. 'And once Craig gets my letter tomorrow, it's Dave who should be concerned about his future.'

Chapter 15

Good enough!

That afternoon, 4.45 p.m.

'Hello, Chris, good to see you again,' began Steve, extending a hand to his old university friend.

'And you, Steve,' Chris replied, pulling up a seat. 'Well, have you had a chance to talk all this over with Lynn?'

'More than that,' replied Steve. 'We've decided together it's the right move for me.'

'That's great. You can even live with the lower basic salary then?' Chris probed.

'Absolutely,' laughed Steve. 'And I've told Lynn we'll be going on a Caribbean cruise next Christmas when I get the first big bonus through.'

'Well, I'm sure you'll be looking out the Panama hat before the year's out,' joked Chris. 'And we'd review your salary for the New Year. So you can start in a month's time then?'

'Yes, my resignation is in and I'm free to start then,' replied Steve.

'That's great,' began Chris. 'Oh, just one thing. The car we give to our Sales Director is a Ford Mondeo.'

'A Mondeo?' asked Steve, hesitatingly.

'A Mondeo Ghia. Is that OK?' enquired Chris.

'That's absolutely fine,' smiled Steve, adding to himself: 'For now!'

Saturday 18 February, 11.15 a.m.

Steve put another round of toast in front of Lynn as they sat at the breakfast bar.

'You know, this flat's getting a bit small for us,' began Lynn, 'especially if we want a little brother or sister for Nicky to play with sometime soon.'

Steve freeze-framed his bite on a piece of toast for dramatic effect.

'Well, if I don't get this promotion, there's nothing to stop me – is there?' Lynn continued.

'Do I sense a little hint of defeatism?' suggested Steve.

'Just being realistic,' replied Lynn. 'There were several other good candidates in for the job and I thought I'd have heard by now if I'd got it.'

The sound of the letterbox rattling stopped the conversation.

Steve returned from the hallway with several envelopes in his hand.

'This, I believe, is for you, Lynn,' he said. 'Looks as if it's from the training department.'

'You open it, Steve,' she suggested.

'Come on, it's your moment,' retorted Steve.

Hesitatingly, Lynn lifted a knife and slit the letter open. She read the first two lines and shrieked in delight, throwing her arms round her husband.

'I take it you're the new Head of Training?' Steve asked, grinning widely. 'And that any thoughts of an addition to the family are on hold?'

'I suppose so,' replied Lynn. 'Unless I find within a few months that I can't ...'

'Stop it,' interrupted Steve. 'You'll be just fine.'

'It is a very responsible post,' replied Lynn.

'And you're a very capable person,' countered Steve.

'You're right. I realize that now,' said Lynn.

'Yeah, you've come quite a way in the past few months,' suggested Steve.

'We both have,' replied Lynn. 'But what's been so different recently?'

'We've talked a lot more, Lynn,' said Steve. 'Sometimes argued – but we've worked things out.'

'So what got us talking?' asked Lynn.

'Well those bizarre texts stirred things up a bit, didn't they?' replied Steve.

'Now there's a thing,' continued Lynn. 'Remember how we couldn't delete them? Well I looked through my texts yesterday and there was no sign of them.'

'Strange,' said Steve. 'I'll check mine.'

After repeatedly scrolling through his texts, Steve reported back: 'No, they've gone!'

'Damn! And I'd promised Helena that I'd show her all the questions when we meet for coffee next week,' began Lynn. 'What on earth were they now?'

Steve opened a kitchen drawer and pulled out a paper and pen.

'I'm sure we'll remember them, if we just go through them one by one,' he said. 'You got the first one. What was it?'

'ARE YOU HUNGRY FOR LOVE?' replied Lynn.

'And how did you respond to that?' asked Steve.

'Well, at first I really didn't think I was comfort eating – but I was,' began Lynn. 'I felt lonely in the evenings and we were both caught up in our own worlds and had drifted apart. But it made me realize that I was using food as a substitute – and what I needed was to feel better about myself – and us – rather than try to feel better by snacking.

'I needed to satisfy my emotional hunger – and now I feel better about myself and us.'

'What was your first text?' she asked.

'ARE YOU GOOD ENOUGH?' he replied.

'And what did you do about that?' she asked.

'Well, at first I was really hacked off,' he replied. 'It came when all the problems with the Bulldog were getting out of hand. I was feeling bad enough already without that nonsense.'

'But didn't it make you start to think about the causes of that?' asked Lynn.

'Sure,' he replied. 'I started to realize I was far too hard on myself. I'd always looked for my dad's approval – but never got it. So I suppose I began to understand that I only need to approve of myself – and value myself for being a worthy human being.

'What other people think of me has become far less important. It's what I think of myself that really counts.'

'That's so true,' said Lynn. 'And my next text got me thinking along similar lines. Do you remember, it was: IS YOUR EMOTIONAL BANK BALANCE IN THE RED? At first, it really upset me. But I was allowing myself to be used by everybody and couldn't say no to anybody.'

'Remember we looked at the pizzas,' recalled Steve, 'and re-divided your time to leave some left over for you?'

'Yes,' began Lynn. 'I hadn't realized how much I needed to feel liked by everybody – but, I just needed to like myself more. And funnily enough, I feel so much better for having more time for me.

'You've really got to keep your emotional bank balance in credit – by investing enough time and energy in looking after yourself.'

'Quite right!' said Steve. 'And you're looking so much happier since you started doing that.'

'Your next text was something about bullies, wasn't it?' asked Lynn.

'WHO ARE THE BULLIES IN YOUR LIFE?' replied Steve. 'And I began to realize that I was being bullied by the Bulldog – and was still being bullied by my dad, in a way. I'd never challenged Dad's criticism. In fact, I'd adopted it and come to believe it. I even realized I was bullying myself!

'Once I'd realized who the bullies were, I could challenge them for the first time in my life.'

'Hey, Steve, remember that time we were getting stuck into the garden and that message came through: WHO ARE YOU PRUNING BACK TO PROMOTE HEALTHY GROWTH?'

'Of course,' began Steve, 'the day Helena and Jim were pruned back and Andrea and Bob were weeded out.'

'Yeah, that was a laugh,' began Lynn, 'but our friendships had really become far too cluttered. And we've now given ourselves room to breathe – and grow. I was expecting a backlash, but some of them probably feel the benefit too.

'Ultimately, you have to keep all relationships balanced, healthy – and under review. That's how to flourish and grow with the people you choose to have in your life.'

Steve fell quiet.

'What's up?' asked Lynn.

'Oh nothing,' said Steve. 'It's just that I was in a bad way at the time I got the next message: HAVE YOU LOST YOUR BEARINGS? It was the day I'd had a bust-up with the Bulldog. I went for a few drinks too many – and I thought about driving the car into a brick wall.'

'You thought about killing yourself?' Lynn gasped.

'I was just feeling sorry for myself,' retreated Steve. 'I'd had too much to drink.'

'Steve, promise me you'll never bottle things up like that again,' pleaded Lynn.

'No, I won't,' he began. 'But, you know, it was a turning point for me. I really had been feeling lost and heading nowhere. But that Confidence Compass you'd found pointed me in the right direction. I really had no idea how "driven" I was – constantly working harder to feel better about myself. And the truth is, I was on a downward spiral.

'I now feel I'm heading in the right direction – balancing all the hard work with a much greater belief in myself.'

'I was having an awful day myself,' said Lynn, 'when my next text came through. I'd fallen out with Mum – and Nicky was playing up in the supermarket when I got a message: WHO ARE YOUR ROLE MODELS? It got me thinking about Dad and all his broken promises – and Mum had a dig at me for paying too much attention to celebrities and their lifestyles.'

'She had a point, Lynn' suggested Steve.

'I know she did,' replied Lynn. 'I just wasn't ready to admit it. But I now pay far less attention to who people are – and far more attention to what they believe and what they do.

'I now choose my role models for their depth of character, rather than their superficial image.'

'Your mum had a pop at your parenting skills that day, as I recall,' said Steve, 'and that's what my next message was about: WHO ARE YOU PARENTING? When we talked about it – or argued about it, to be more accurate – you accused me of being too hard on Nicky and I accused you of being too soft. In the end, we just had to learn to be firm – and set clear boundaries. We were guilty

of sending him mixed messages. So we both had to sing from the same song sheet.

'I certainly didn't realize that I was being so critical of him. And I now make a point of telling him how much I love him. I now also know that I can be a parent to myself – and treat myself in the way any good parent would treat their child.'

'It was New Year's Day when I got the next message,' said Lynn, *'HOW ARE YOU COPING WITH CHANGE?'*

'So it was,' said Steve. *'The day I heard that Mum had died.'*

'We were driving to Irene and Ian's,' said Lynn. *'And worried about whether they'd be put out by us seeing less of them – and we arrived to hear that awful news.*

'I think I'd been rather afraid of change in the past. But now I realize you have to swim with the tide of change – rather than against the current.

'In fact, I'd always thought that I would make changes ONCE I felt more confident. But it's the other way round. I feel more confident BECAUSE I've made changes.'

'Well, the big change I made around that time was to my language,' said Steve. *'I had been so negative about Mum's funeral – but that message WHAT DO YOUR WORDS SAY ABOUT YOU? certainly addressed that.'*

'And I was being unfair to myself by watering down my attributes whenever I spoke,' added Lynn.

'And you would never accept a compliment,' continued Steve.

'Do you still think it's phoney to say "I'm good" instead of "Not bad" when people ask how you are, Steve?' asked Lynn.

'No, I've just got used to it – and I feel I'm being more positive with Nicky,' said Steve.

'It's easy to change your words as the first step to thinking, feeling and acting more positively. Positive words also help to challenge that critical voice in your head.'

'Remember we used role play to practise your positive responses to the Bulldog?' asked Lynn. 'That worked a treat. But what was the message that prompted it?'

'HOW ARE YOU AT SOLVING PROBLEMS?' replied Steve.

'Of course,' continued Lynn. 'And we addressed your biggest problem by working out a plan to deal with Dave face to face without him beating you down.'

'I reckon I'd been running away from the problem until then,' confessed Steve. 'It was only when I faced up to it and understood it that I could start to deal with it.

'It's only when you ask yourself the right questions that you can bring the problem into sharp focus – and you can find a way forward.'

'Then I got the message asking ARE YOU ACTING AS IF?' said Lynn. 'And I had no idea what it was about. By that time, you'd had to act as if you were really confident going into the meeting with Dave – but then you'd prepared well and you pulled off a good performance.'

'You're forgetting one thing,' teased Steve.

'What?' asked Lynn.

'A confident manner!' Steve reminded her. 'You have to look as if you're confident to feel as if you are.'

'Well, I certainly used that when I went for the new job,' said Lynn. 'And it worked a treat.

'And if you keep on looking and acting more confident, you become more confident. And when you feel more confident, you look and act more confident. It's an upward spiral.'

'Well, your confidence certainly took an upward turn this week with the way you handled that job interview,' said Steve. 'But it was a strange message you got before it: DOES YOUR MIND WORK FOR YOU?'

'Yes, by the time I got there,' said Lynn, 'the only person who had to be convinced that I had a good chance of getting the job was me.'

'So what made the difference?' asked Steve.

'I just silenced my "goblin" and started saying what I believed to be true,' she replied. 'I suppose I put my mind to work for me, rather than against me.

'You really do have to make your mind your best friend if you want to find peace of mind.'

'I wonder about your mind sometimes,' said Steve, 'given that you saw the interviewers with Mickey Mouse ears and in their pyjamas.'

'You're one to mock,' said Lynn. 'You saw Dave in his boxer shorts and with huge ears.'

'Which he has anyway!' they said in unison.

'Well, you won't have to look at them for much longer,' suggested Lynn as the laughter subsided.

'True,' said Steve. 'I'll miss Dave – but not much!'

'Will anything happen to him when Craig reacts to your letter?'
asked Lynn.

'Who knows?' said Steve. 'But if everybody else in the sales team
is spared his bullying, that would be a good thing.'

Lynn paused.

'So why have the text messages disappeared?' she asked. 'And
does that mean they've stopped?'

'I don't know,' said Steve. 'I really don't know.'

Monday 20 March, 8.50 a.m.

Dave the Bulldog trudged wearily into the hotel foyer and scanned
the conference board to find the right suite.

He and four others would be spending the next six hours on an
'Effective Communications' course, organized by Craig for 'se-
lected' managers.

Craig had looked closely at his senior management team and
decided that some would benefit from a few reminders on how
to communicate positively with staff.

Dave went to switch off his mobile, but a bleep indicated he had
one new message to check first.

It read:

Are you good enough?

Index